I heartily recommend this book not only as a history of the World Convention, but as a very helpful introduction to the work of the Stone-Campbell Movement itself. Based on a superb acquaintance with the sources, it excels in every way. Holloway rightly sees the Restoration Movement as a global fellowship rather than an exclusively American one. Stone-Campbell Christians will find this book to be an indispensable guide to the movement's history, especially over the last century. Dr. Holloway, the World Convention, and all those involved in producing this meaningful volume are to be sincerely congratulated.

 —**Dyron B. Daughrity,** Professor of Religion, Pepperdine University

No one knows the history of the World Convention of Churches of Christ better than Dr. Gary Holloway, Executive Director since 2010. Through careful study of the ministry's archives, Holloway has provided readers with a deeply insightful and sometimes surprising overview of this global ministry—from its backgrounds and beginning in 1930, through the 20th century, to the amazing developments of the 21st century. The core commitment of World Convention has remained the same—the visible unity of followers of Christ. With the shift of the majority of members of Stone-Campbell churches to the global south, the current chapter of the story of World Convention provides new and exciting opportunities to model that unity. This volume provides a solid foundation for seizing those opportunities.

 —**Douglas A. Foster,** Professor of Church History,
 Abilene Christian University

This new history of the World Convention is a candid, richly and fascinatingly detailed account of the ongoing evolution of an organization formed to advance the visible unity and witness of the church through a global fellowship of Christians of the Stone-Campbell Movement; an important contribution to our understanding of this movement!

 —**D. Newell Williams,** President and Professor of Church History,
 Brite Divinity School

Holloway's lively account of the World Convention helps contemporary readers to relive the exuberant atmosphere of its assemblies throughout the history, as well as to appreciate its visionary leaders who overcame formidable challenges. Overall, this book is a godsend for those who seek to understand how the particularity of the Stone-Campbell fellowship can lead to promote the global unity of all Christians.

—**Yukikazu Obata,** Ibaraki Christian University, Japan

Within the pages of this book, Gary Holloway examines the growth, development, and ministry of the World Convention of Churches of Christ from its beginning until the present. As a service to the three major streams of the Stone-Campbell Movement, the World Convention reminds us of the unity our movement's forefathers sought and their desire to see Christianity spread throughout the entire world. While the valuable work of the World Convention has tended to be overlooked by many within the Stone-Campbell Movement, it is hoped that this book will raise up a greater awareness of the World Convention and its important ministry.

—**Rick Cherok,** Professor of Church History,
Cincinnati Christian University

This book contains a concise and well-told history of the World Convention of Churches of Christ, from the nascent vision provided by Jesse Bader to the Convention's historic first meeting in Asia (Damoh, India) in 2017. With this offering, Gary Holloway, historian and current Executive Director of the World Convention, provides a significant gift for both the churches affiliated with the Stone-Campbell Movement and those active in the global ecumenical movement. In pages recounting accomplishments and challenges, cooperative efforts and significant tensions, consistency and innovation, this narrative conveys the story of faith finding expression in the midst of diverse cultures, and the struggle of people, programs, publications, and prayer to give life to prospects found in the Stone-Campbell commitment to Christian unity across both decades and globe.

—**Mark G. Toulouse,** Principal, Emmanuel College of Victoria University
in the University of Toronto

In a world where the words "independent" and "individual" are considered sacred, the concept of fellowship provides a glimpse of the glory of the unity and solidarity that the Lord intended for His Church. We must never forget that Jesus said that our love for one another would be a witness to the world of not only who we are but of our relationship to Him. This is what World Convention embodies. As was said at the assembly of the 1984 convention, the World Convention is a 'tower of unity'. Gary Holloway's dual work on both the history of the Restoration Movement (beautifully and concisely presented), and his detailed history of the World Convention and its Global Gatherings (new name) made me freshly proud of my own heritage in that movement and excited me as to what the World Convention stands for – fellowship and unity and global mission. The visible expression of the Convention, the Global Gatherings, are just the 'glamourous' part of something that has much deeper meaning and purpose. The three historic streams of the Restoration movement can be proud of what the World Convention means to our fellowship and where it is heading in pursuing our ancient quest for unity. Thank you Gary for your tremendous presentation of the World Convention's history and exciting future.

   —**Leonard Thompson—Director,** Strategic World Evangelism,
   Chennai, India

A GLOBAL FELLOWSHIP

A GLOBAL FELLOWSHIP

A Concise History
of the World Convention of
Churches of Christ

GARY HOLLOWAY

World Convention
CHRISTIAN · CHURCHES OF CHRIST · DISCIPLES OF CHRIST

A GLOBAL FELLOWSHIP
A Concise History of the World Convention of Churches of Christ

ISBN 978-0-9989164-0-8

To Richard and Esther Spellman,
and to all who are partners in the ministry
of World Convention.

Contents

Introduction

The Stone-Campbell Movement began as a Christian renewal movement in the early nineteenth century, led by Barton Stone and Thomas and Alexander Campbell. The roots of the churches from that movement—known as Churches of Christ, the Christian Church (Disciples of Christ), and Christian Churches and Churches of Christ are nineteenth century attempts at Christian renewal in England, the Commonwealth Countries, and in the United States. See Gary Holloway and Douglas A. Foster, *Renewing the World: A Concise Global History of the Stone-Campbell Movement* (Abilene: ACU Press 2015), and D. Newell Williams, Douglas A. Foster, and Paul M. Blowers, *The Stone-Campbell Movement: A Global History* (St Louis: Chalice Press, 2013), for more on the history of the Movement.

Three earlier works, an M.A. thesis at Butler University by Ronald I. W. Hurst in 1964, a brief history, *Together in Christ: a*

History of the World Convention of Churches of Christ 1930–2008, by Clinton J Holloway, and "The World Convention of Churches of Christ: Connecting the Stone-Campbell Movement Globally," *Stone-Campbell Journal* 19:2 (Fall 2016) have told the story of the one organization that has sought since 1930 to bring together this group of churches. Based on the organization's archives, this book, although concise, attempts to give a fuller account of the World Convention of Churches of Christ that also gives these churches a seat at the table with other Christian World Communions, praying and working to fulfil the prayer of Jesus that all who believe may be one so that the world may believe.

Background and Preparation

The World Convention of Churches of Christ serves a group of churches found in 199 countries and territories with a total of around 10 million adherents worldwide. The roots of those churches are in nineteenth century movements in England, the Commonwealth Countries, and in the United States. The first "founding document" of that history is *The Last Will and Testament of the Springfield Presbytery* written in Kentucky in 1804. The ministers who wrote those words began the first group of independent churches in this Movement. Led by Barton W. Stone (1772–1844) and others, those Christian Churches or Churches of Christ (both names were used) wanted to go back to the Bible for the sake of Christian unity, so that the world might come to believe in Christ.

Although many before him called Christians back to the Bible for the sake of Christian unity, Thomas Campbell's publication of *The Declaration and Address* in 1809 marked a significant intellectual beginning to this Movement. Along with his son, Alexander

Campbell (1788–1866), and Walter Scott (1796–1861), an evangelist, Thomas Campbell (1763–1854) led a group of congregations generally known as the Disciples of Christ that grew considerably in southern Ohio and western Virginia.

Meanwhile, in England, William James of London began publishing the *Millennial Harbinger* in 1835, reprinting some of the articles of Alexander Campbell. In 1836, James Wallis of Nottingham and others formed the first Church of Christ in Great Britain. Soon there were congregations throughout the United Kingdom. Later those churches spread from Britain to Australia and New Zealand.

In 1832, most of those in the Stone group and the Campbell group in the United States began to merge. In spite of significant differences between the two groups, they also had much in common. They were committed to the Scriptures as the only true source of spiritual light, life, and authority. They were committed to ending the shameful divisions among followers of Christ, and therefore opposed anything that separated Christians including creeds, clergy, unscriptural names, and denominational bodies. They believed that the church depicted in the New Testament was the ideal church, pure and free from all the corruptions of the ages. Restoring that unified church was one of their goals.

That unified Stone-Campbell Movement (as historians call it) grew rapidly on the American frontier. The congregations in the movement went by different names—Disciples of Christ, Christian Churches, and Churches of Christ—but maintained a single sense of identity.

That unity began to break down around the time of the Civil War. The ill feelings caused by the War, along with differences on theological issues like missionary societies, instrumental music in worship, the role of the local preacher, and other subjects soon led to a major division. Most in the north became known as Disciples of Christ or Christian Churches. Most in the south took the name

Churches of Christ. Some place that division in 1889, when Daniel Sommer (1850–1940) and others called for a break of fellowship in the "Address and Declaration" at Sand Creek, Illinois. The "official" date of that division (according to a government religious census) is 1906.

In the twentieth century, Disciples of Christ divided again, eventually forming two groups. One is the Christian Church (Disciples of Christ) which restructured in 1968 with three expressions of church—congregational, regional, and general. The Christian Churches/Churches of Christ (both names are used) are more conservative and strictly congregational in organization. Thus, there are three large Christian groups in America today with their roots in the Stone-Campbell Movement (also known as the Restoration Movement).

Conventions and Conferences

The Stone-Campbell Movement has always emphasized the importance of congregational independence. The first meetings beyond the congregational level were state conventions, usually held annually, beginning in the 1830s. The first national convention was the American Christian Missionary Society meeting October 23, 1849. 156 delegates from eleven states met in Cincinnati. Alexander Campbell did not attend because of ill health but was elected the first President. There was opposition to the American Christian Missionary Society from the beginning. That opposition intensified during and after the Civil War and was one of the major issues that separated Disciples of Christ from Churches of Christ.

In part to blunt that opposition, a new plan was adopted at the 1869 convention in Louisville, Kentucky. The Louisville Plan created a General Christian Missionary Convention based on paid congregational membership with official delegates. At first the Louisville Plan had widespread support but the concepts of official delegates and specific dues led to its demise in 1895. However, by 1917, the International Convention ("International" because it included Canada and the United States) was formed with official delegates from congregations and agencies of the church. That same year African American Disciples organized the National Christian Missionary Convention. In 1968, Disciples restructured into the Christian Church (Disciples of Christ) with a biennial delegate General Assembly. In 1969, the National Christian Missionary Convention merged with the Christian Church (Disciples of Christ) but kept their own biennial gathering as the National Convocation of the Christian Church (Disciples of Christ).

Concerns about the power of extra-congregational organizations and issues over how to do missionary work led some to begin the North American Christian Convention in 1927. This is a gathering open to all who wish to attend with no official delegates.

Churches of Christ in the United States have never had official delegate conventions but do have annual lectureships sponsored by Church of Christ colleges and also other large gatherings, open to all. These large meetings with thousands in attendance, where theological topics are discussed, have great influence among those churches.

Thus in the United States and Canada, there have been state, regional, and national gatherings from the 1830s.[1] Stone-Campbell churches in other parts of the world also developed conventions and conferences. British churches began a "Co-operation Meeting" in 1842. In 1881 a separate Christian Association was formed. These two organizations reunited in 1917 as a national Conference. Australian churches established state conferences beginning in the 1860s

---

[1] For more information, see "Conventions" in *The Encyclopedia of the Stone-Campbell Movement,* Douglas Foster, and et.al. editors (Grand Rapids: Eerdmans, 2004).

and held their first Federal Conference in 1906. In the late nineteenth
century, churches in New Zealand
began district conferences. The first
Dominion Conference, encom-
passing all the churches, was held
in Wellington in 1901, becoming
annual after World War I.

Through mission efforts, by
1930, Churches of Christ or Christian Churches had expanded from
the United States, Great Britain,
Canada, Australia, and New Zealand to a total of over thirty coun-

Billy Graham and Jesse Bader

tries on every continent. What had not been attempted before 1930
was to have a worldwide conference of the churches, open to all.

Preparation

The World Convention of Churches of Christ had its inception in
the heart of one man, Jesse Moran Bader (1886–1963). Bader was a
Disciple minister to churches in Kansas and Missouri before serving in France and Germany with the Y.M.C.A. during World War
I. His wife, Golda Maud Elam, became a noted leader in United
Church Women. In 1920 he became the Secretary of Evangelism
of the United Christian Missionary Society.

His passion for worldwide evangelism led him in 1924 to con-
ceive of a global meeting of Churches of Christ (as most congregations of the Stone-Campbell Movement were called). In 1925, he
visited the Conference of the Churches of Christ in Great Britain,
proposing the idea of a World Convention in 1930 to coincide
with the 1900th year of Pentecost. The British responded with
enthusiasm. As a result, when the International Convention met in

Memphis in 1926, a Pentecost Committee of Fifteen was appointed to plan for a celebration in 1930. At the first meeting of that committee, Bader was appointed Executive Secretary, and the committee recommended that a World Convention be held in Washington D.C. in 1930. A World Convention committee was appointed, eventually having sixty members from 27 countries.

That committee, called the Program Committee, did most of its work through a Central Committee of twelve with Bader as chair. In 1927, Bader made a two month trip to promote the Convention in Australia and New Zealand. In June of 1928, Bader visited the Fourth Baptist World Congress in Toronto, Canada to see how such a gathering might be organized.

From 1928 to the opening of the Washington Convention, the program committee met frequently, making decisions on the venues, program, speakers, music, meals, travel arrangements and a myriad of other details. Some of these meetings were held jointly with the planning committee for the International Convention which would also be held in Washington preceding the World Convention. A publicity committee worked hard, spending $1660 to print 750,000 gummed stickers with the dates for the convention. These, along with 2000 posters, were distributed through the churches, particularly in the United States.

Challenges

World Convention faced challenges from the world economic situation and from tensions within the Stone-Campbell Movement. The stock market crash of October 1929 ushered in the Great Depression. Although the full effects of the Depression would be felt after 1930, financial difficulties did hamper planning for the World Convention in Washington for 1930. As late as February 1930, Bader and other organizers were anticipating attendance at 15,000 to 25,000 for the International Convention and the World Convention. However, attendance was around 6300. The lower attendance was in part because financial difficulties kept many from attending. What did it cost to attend? First there were travel costs to Washington. The twenty-four Convention hotels ranged in price from $4 to $12 per night ($58 to $172 in 2017 dollars). The registration fee was $1 per person ($14 in 2017 dollars). In addition there was the cost of meals, sightseeing, and other sundries.

Of course transportation costs were higher for those outside the United States since it required for most a long steamship voyage. For example, the cost for travel from Australia, rail travel across the United States, and return to Australia was 148 Australia pounds or $740 in 1930 (equal to $10,645 in 2017 dollars). From Great Britain the cost was 55 pounds, which equals $3955 today. Those from outside the United States were not required to pay the $1 registration fee and most were housed for free in the homes of Washington area Christians. A World Convention Committee for Bringing Nationals to Washington was formed to raise money to help attendees from outside the United States, but few funds were raised. As Bader replied to the request of I.S. Prokhanoff of Russia for funds to help in travel, ". . . no funds are available. The World Convention Program Committee is finding it difficult to finance the convention itself. . . ."[2]

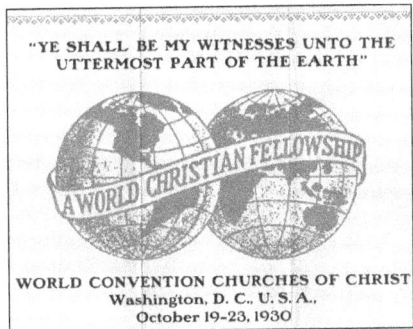

"YE SHALL BE MY WITNESSES UNTO THE UTTERMOST PART OF THE EARTH"

A WORLD CHRISTIAN FELLOWSHIP

WORLD CONVENTION CHURCHES OF CHRIST
Washington, D. C., U. S. A.,
October 19-23, 1930

Poster Washington Convention

However, in spite of the financial challenges, when the Convention ended, H.H. Peters as Treasurer of the Pentecost Anniversary Observance (which financed the World Convention)

---

[2] Letter from Jesse Bader to I.S. Prokhanoff, January 6, 1930.

could report a balance of $229 in the treasury. The Central Committee of the World Convention received this report "with great joy."[3]

The other great challenge facing the First World Convention was division within the Stone-Campbell Movement. A long process of division beginning after the Civil War resulted in Churches of Christ being listed separately from Disciples of Christ in the United States Religious Census of 1906. In the first few decades of the twentieth century, Churches of Christ developed a sectarian identity and wanted little to do with the Christian Churches (Disciples). However, Jesse Bader asked George A. Kingman, minister of the Fourteenth Street Church of Christ in Washington to be on the Program Committee for the World Convention in Washington. Kingman declined. Bader then wrote Kingman, asking him for a list of preachers from Churches of Christ who might be persuaded to attend the Convention. Kingman sent a list of twenty-three names, including G.C Brewer, R.H. Boll, and Henry Speck.[4] However, none of them appeared on the Convention program, and there is no record of them, except for Klingman, attending.

A second division among American Disciples was also occurring. The issues included the place of higher criticism of the Bible, how to be involved in the ecumenical movement, and how to do mission work. There was criticism of the United Christian Missionary Society along with charges that some of their missionaries practiced "open membership," that is allowing the unimmersed to be members. These tensions led to some Disciples, known as Cooperatives, supporting the UCMS and others (Independents) doing missions through direct support of

---

[3] Minutes of the Meeting of the Central Committee of the World Convention of Churches of Christ, LaSalle Hotel, Chicago, December 19, 1930.

[4] Letter from George A. Klingman to Jesse Bader, June 25, 1929.

missionaries by congregations. The Independents established their own gathering, the North American Christian Convention, which met first in 1927 in Indianapolis.

Eventually these tensions would result in two fellowships—the Christian Church (Disciples of Christ) and the Christian Churches/Churches of Christ. However in 1930, there was still widespread feeling that the Disciples (Cooperatives and Independents) were a single fellowship. World Convention worked to promote this feeling of unity by including leaders from both groups on the Program Committee. For example, P.H. Welshimer, who was President of the North American Christian Convention in 1927 and 1929, was on the World Convention Program Committee from its beginning. Welshimer wrote Bader, "I trust we shall be able in the World Convention program committee to build a program that will be accepted by all our people . . ."[5] It is significant that there was no North American Christian Convention in 1930. Leaders hoped all would attend the World Convention.

However, strong disapproval of the program came from Edwin Errett of Standard Publishing. As a leader of the Independents, Errett felt that the proposed program did not focus on the particular doctrines of the Restoration Movement, asking . . . "Where is there revealed anything of our distinctive message in the program?"[6] He also objected to specific speakers as "liberal" and asked . . . "how much of this program could not be just as well used by one of the denominations?"[7] Errett's criticisms are odd in light of the two page article in the printed World Convention program entitled, "The Restoration Movement—Its Beginnings and Ideals."

---

[5] Letter from P.H. Welshimer to Jesse Bader, October 17, 1929.
[6] Letter from Edwin Errett to P.H. Welshimer, December 25,1929
[7] Ibid

Interestingly, the World Convention also faced criticism that it was "dominated by the Standard group."[8]

Divisiveness also plagued the movement in Great Britain. Although there were tensions there also over the higher criticism of the Bible, the primary issue was over open or close communion. The majority of congregations in Great Britain favored close communion where only baptized believers were permitted to partake of the Lord's Supper. This topic was discussed thoroughly at the 1929 and 1930 conferences of the British churches. The disagreement may have prevented some from Great Britain from attending the World Convention in 1930. It even divided families, with R.W. Black leading the Twynholm church (the largest congregation of Churches of Christ in Britain at the time) to join the Baptist Union in 1831, partly because the Baptists practiced close communion. His brother, J.W. Black, remained with Churches of Christ and was a prominent leader on the Program Committee of the World Convention in 1930 and was the President of the 1935 World Convention in Leicester, England.

Divisiveness in the United States and in Great Britain did not deter Bader and others from working for an inclusive convention. "This convention takes in all our people without reference to shades of theology, geography, color, race, or language," wrote Bader.[9] He later added, "The World Convention is not controlled by any group, it is not held in ignorance of any group and is not for the propaganda of any group. It is a great fellowship for mutual helpfulness and acquaintance."[10]

---

[8] Letter from W.J. Lhamon to Jesse Bader, September 5, 1930

[9] Letter from Jesse Bader to W.J. Lhamon, August 27, 1930

[10] Letter from Jesse Bader to W.J. Lhamon, September 10, 1930

Beginnings:
Washington and Leicester

The first World Convention was held immediately after the International Convention of Disciples of Christ (the name of the United States and Canadian Convention of Disciples) had met in Washington, D.C., October 14–19, 1930. This assured a good attendance for the World Convention since many attendees of the International Convention stayed for the joint Communion service of the two conventions on Sunday afternoon.

The First World Convention, Washington, D.C., October 19–23, 1930

Since the anticipated attendance was too large for one venue in Washington at the time, this Convention was unusual in that it had its program simultaneously in two venues, the Washington Auditorium at 19th and E Streets NW, and at Constitution Hall at 18th and D Streets NW. Washington Auditorium had opened in 1925, seating 6000. It served as a site for conventions, sports and

Registration for Washington Convention

arts programs, and even Franklin Roosevelt's inaugural ball in 1933. In 1935 it was converted to office space used by various Federal agencies. It was demolished in 1963 and is now an extension of Rawlins Park. Constitution Hall, seating 4000, opened in 1929 to house the annual meeting of the Daughters of the Revolution. It is still used today for arts programs and lectures.

The first World Convention opened Sunday, October 19, 1930 with a communion service at those two venues and at the newly built National City Christian Church at Thomas Circle. Admission was by ticket at National City but open at the other two venues. Over 6500 registered for the Convention, and over 6300 were present at one of the three communion services. Bader estimated that 10,000 to 12,000 were present for at least part of the program.

The evening session began at 7:30 with Jesse Bader presiding at Washington Auditorium and Charles Medbury presiding at Constitution Hall. At the front of each hall was a large banner with the theme for the entire Convention: "Ye Shall Be My Witnesses—Unto the Uttermost Part of the Earth." Cloyd

Goodnight, President of Bethany College, presented a gavel made from wood from the Brush Run Church to Jesse Bader as a symbol of the office of President of World Convention. Following the theme of "Deepening World Fellowship Among Churches of Christ," the program at both venues consisted of a roll call of the thirty nations where there were churches of the Stone-Campbell Movement.[11] A representative of each nation marched in with their national flag and made a three minute presentation on their national churches. Twenty-one nations were represented by native citizens, while speakers from Britain, Australia, and New Zealand, and the United States presented for the others. Ludwig von Gertell made the most touching presentation. Representing the German churches he said, "My country has had two flags. I bring to the World Convention greetings from the churches in my homeland and say to you that the flag of the German Republic is the flag of peace!" Gertell was referring to the flags of the German Empire and of the Weimar Republic. In light of the recent German election of September 14, 1930, where the Nazi party became the second largest in the Reichstag, Gertell's assurance of peace met with a loud cheer from the Convention.[12] After the national presentations, the session ended with the assembly singing "Blest Be the Tie that Binds" in their own national language.

Monday morning's theme was "Our Book of Beginnings." Speakers recounted the early history of the Stone-Campbell Movement in Great Britain, New Zealand, Australia, the United States, and

---

[11] Great Britain, Canada, Australia, New Zealand, New Hebrides, Siam, Rhodesia, South Africa, Nyasaland, Belgian Congo, Japan, Jamaica, Russia, Mexico, Paraguay, Hawaii, Estonia, Latvia, Palestine, Puerto Rico, Korea, Germany, Tibet, Denmark, Philippines, India, China, Poland, and the United States.

[12] Willard Shelton, "Highlights of the Conventions," *Christian-Evangelist* (October 30, 1930), 1435.

1930—White House and Herbert Hoover

Canada. One session focused on early missionary efforts, particularly the work of the American Christian Missionary Society. Monday afternoon centered on evangelism, Bible schools, efforts at Christian unity, publications, and leadership as "Achievements of a Century." A brief World Convention business session was held Monday afternoon, where the recommendation was made for a World Convention in Leicester, England in 1935 and officers were chosen for that Convention. Two substantive resolutions were also approved, one condemning war and one supporting the national prohibition of alcohol. Monday evening was the Australia-New Zealand Dinner for attendees from those nations. Monday evening's addresses were on "The Church Invincible." Thus Monday was a retelling of the Stone-Campbell story in a decidedly triumphalistic fashion. One highlight at the Washington Auditorium was a brief reminiscence by Campbell Jones, aged 91, of Wheeling, West Virginia of hearing Alexander Campbell preach in 1859.

"Pentecost Among the Nations" was the theme Tuesday morning, October 21, since 1930 was a celebration of the 1900th anniversary of the Pentecost after the resurrection. The program consisted of reports from twelve nations on the current state of church growth. The Pentecost theme was continued with a prayer service entitled "With the Early Disciples in an Upper Room Fellowship of Prayer." Prayer, particularly prayer for evangelism, was an important part of the Convention with a prayer room open daily from 8 a.m. to 9 p.m..

After the morning session was the All-Nations luncheon at the Mayflower Hotel, near the White House, with 1377 in attendance. The program consisted of 26 speakers who, in one minute each, addressed, "The Greatest Thing Our Churches are Doing." It was originally hoped that President Herbert Hoover would address the Convention on opening night, but since that was not possible because of his schedule, on Tuesday afternoon, President Hoover hosted about 5000 Convention delegates at a tea on the White House lawn. This invitation reflects Hoover's Quaker spirituality, the simplicity of the times in 1930 (with few worries about Presidential security), and the significance of the Disciples and other Christian denominations as a political force.

The Pension Fund of Disciples of Christ provided a complimentary dinner for attendees from outside the United States. This began a long tradition of support for World Convention from the Pension Fund. Tuesday evening's sessions were on Christian unity with addresses on the plea for Christian unity and the purpose of Christian unity.

All day Wednesday, the theme was "Present Day Affirmations of our Christian Faith." The presentations were on contextual theology, on how the gospel is to be understood in various cultures. Presentations were made from Japan, China, India, Africa (called "The Dark Continent"), the Philippines, Continental Europe, Mexico, South America (Paraguay), Jamaica, the British Empire, and the United States. Donald Anderson McGavran, who later would be recognized as one of the greatest missiologists of the twentieth century, made the presentation on India. The evening sessions were on World Missions with an address at both venues from John R. Mott, then chairman of the International Missionary Council and president of the World's Alliance of YMCAs. The presence of Mott and of Daniel A. Poling, President of World Christian Endeavor, on the program set a precedent for speakers from outside the Stone-Campbell Movement to be plenary speakers at subsequent World Conventions. Arthur Holmes, the speaker at Constitution Hall the same time as Mott spoke at Washington Auditorium, collapsed ten minutes into his presentation but soon recovered.

Thursday's sessions were held only in Washington Auditorium, with Christian Education the focus of the morning addresses. The Thursday afternoon session tackled contemporary world problems like alcohol abuse, disunity, and war. Kirby Page, who in 1935 would help to found the Disciples Peace Fellowship, gave a passionate address entitled, "A Warless World." The final session of the convention featured an address by Hugh McLellan titled "Crown Him Lord of All," followed appropriately with the singing of the Hallelujah Chorus.

Music played an important role in the Convention. There were musical presentations by over fifty soloists, duets, quartets, as well as by the Convention Chorus of 300 voices. Congregational hymn singing was interspersed between the addresses and sermons. The printed program contained the words of fifty hymns, but no musical notation.

The number and diversity of presiders, speakers, singers, and prayer leaders was staggering. There were 158 named leaders in the program, 126 of them speakers, including 21 women presenters. Presenters came from twenty-one countries. The largest delegations from outside the United States and Canada were from Australia with 42 attendees, Great Britain with 20, and New Zealand with 9. In a typical day of the convention, there would be eight addresses or sermons in the morning session, six in the afternoon, and two in the evening, for a total of sixteen per day, twenty to thirty minutes in length. No wonder that one attendee wrote: "We went to the auditorium to relax. Too many speeches? Yes, but after the first three or four, the saints peacefully slept."[13]

When not attending sessions, attendees could browse the exhibits in the lower level of Washington Auditorium. Fifty-nine spaces were used by seventeen organizations, some of whom continue to this day as entities of the Christian Church (Disciples of Christ) and of Christian Churches/Churches of Christ—Christian Board of Publication, Pension Fund of the Christian Church, Johnson Bible College, and Standard Publishing Company. The largest display was by the United Christian Missionary Society. The Christian Restoration Association, representing direct support missionaries, had a booth. Churches of Christ in Poland, Russia, and Australia had their own displays.

Results
By almost all accounts, the first World Convention was a resounding success in terms of attendance, the diversity of presentations, and the reception by the Stone-Campbell Movement. The general public became more aware of the movement through the 1208 press articles on the Convention, published in papers throughout the country. Perhaps the most satisfying result to Bader and other organizers was the continuation of the World Convention with plans for the 1935 meeting in England.

The Second World Convention, Leicester, England, August 7–12, 1935
Most of the planning for the Leicester Convention was done by the Central Committee on Program and Promotion, appointed from the officers of the World Convention—George Stewart, H.H.

---

[13] B.H. Melton, "After Thoughts of Our Washington Conventions," *Christian-Evangelist* (December 11, 1930), 1620

Peters, Charles S. Medbury, H.B. Holloway, and Jesse Bader as chair—with President J.W. Black as an ex-officio member. They were advised by a larger program committee with representatives of each of the thirty-five nations that had a Stone-Campbell church. Bader had led the World Convention while working full-time as Secretary of Evangelism of the United Christian Missionary Society, headquartered at the Missions building in Indianapolis. In 1932, Bader joined the Commission on Evangelism of the Federal Council of Churches in New York. His office there at the United Charities Building at 105 East 22nd Street became the second World Convention headquarters.

The Central Committee recommended that the churches in the Leicester area not begin their local organization for the Convention until after August 1, 1934. Connections between the American, British, and Australian churches were strengthen by visits from J.W. Black to the International Conference in Indianapolis in 1932 and to the Australian Conference in 1933. Jesse Bader visited the British Conference in Edinburgh in 1934. The British churches decided to hold their 1935 Conference in Leicester immediately preceding the World Convention.

Financing the Convention was a challenge during the Great Depression. The Finance Committee of Bader, Peters, and Holloway meeting in November 26, 1932, said $6000 (equal to $105,212 in 2017) would be needed by mid-1934 to finance the promotion of the Convention. H.H. Peters as Treasurer of World Convention sent letters to 1000 congregations of the Disciples in the United States asking for support. Only sixteen replied, and seven congregations sent or pledged a total of $31 to the Convention. The committee turned to individual donors but there is no record of how much they received. Attending the Convention from the United States or Canada was expensive. H.B. Holloway, the Transportation Secretary, estimated total costs at $272.64 per person from

Indianapolis ($4787 in 2017 dollars). Since this was the middle of the Great Depression, it is amazing that over 440 from the United States were able to make the crossing on the ship Britannic to attend the Convention in England. There was even a World Convention program on the ship with worship, singing, lectures, and films.

Of course, on the ground planning was done by the British churches. President John Wycliffe Black was well respected among all the churches and was a talented organizer. His maternal grandfather was James Wallis, one of the founders of the first Church of Christ in Britain. Hosting the Convention was a major undertaking in a country with 196 congregations and a total of 15,327

1935—Crowd at Leicester Convention

members. Leicester itself had nine congregations with a total membership of about 1600. But the British volunteered in large numbers with 192 people serving on the five local committees and many others helping in various ways, including opening their homes to attendees.

The Program

As in Washington, the Program Committee worked hard to include presenters from all the countries of the Stone-Campbell Movement. While most of the speakers from the United States were "Cooperatives," several well-known "Independents" such as James Deforest Murch and P.H. Welshimer attended. There were no known attendees from American a cappella Churches of Christ. There were 148 presenters on the program, men and women, from all the countries where the church existed.

The Convention was held at De Montfort Hall next to Victoria Park in Leicester, a city of 300,000. The theme was "Go Ye and Make Disciples of All Nations." Attendance was around 2500. Each session began with a fifteen minute devotional message focusing on an evangelistic passage from the Bible. At the opening session on Wednesday afternoon, August 7, 1935, there were messages of welcome given by local political and church leaders. This was followed by the Presidential address of J.W. Black, entitled, "The Obligations, Opportunities, and Objectives of the World Convention." The first of the objectives was "The securing of the world unity of the people of God."

Wednesday evening began with devotions, then a presentation on "The Message of the Churches of Christ for Today" by Raphael Harwood Miller of Washington D.C. This was followed (as in Washington) by the Pageant of the Flags, with the Christian Flag and the Peace Flag being presented, then representatives of each of the thirty-five nations present displayed their national flag and gave a brief word about the churches in their country. As at the Washington Convention, Ludwig von Gertell of Germany caused the most stir by appearing without a flag and explaining, "I could bring the old democratic flag of Germany but that would be considered a personal betrayal of my country. I am not going to use the swastika flag, because I don't believe in the divine mission of Hitler."[14]

A youth breakfast on Thursday, August 8, marked the beginning of the first world gathering of the youth of the Churches of Christ. Led by well-known Disciple educator Cynthia Pearl Maus, the Youth Convention welcomed over two hundred young people from six continents and fifteen countries. Meeting in three breakfast and two tea sessions at Wiggeston Girl's School, a short walk

---

[14] Willard E. Shelton, "The Second World Convention," *Christian-Evangelist* (August 29, 1935), 1123

from De Montfort Hall, the youth heard presentations, then divided into five small groups with adult leaders to discuss. Each of those smaller groups chose one of their number to give a ten minute presentation to the entire Convention on Saturday evening. The main Convention sessions on Thursday morning and afternoon consisted of messages on the state of the churches in Great Britain, Canada, Australia, New Zealand, the United States, Asia, Continental Europe, Africa, Latin America, and the Caribbean. A tea for missionaries followed. Thursday night included an address by Samuel Masih of Bilaspur, India on "What Christ Means to Me."

1935—Samuel Masih, Herbert Abao, C.C. Roberts, and Fay Livengood

Friday morning presentations focused on building up the church. Friday afternoon saw three addresses on Christian Unity by F. Luke Wiseman of the Methodist Church in England, Homer W. Carpenter of American Disciples, and W.R. Matthews, Dean of St Paul's in London. This continued the practice of the Washington Convention of having speakers from outside the Stone-Campbell Movement.

Saturday morning's themes were education and the home. The afternoon focused on world peace. There was also a brief memorial service for three recently deceased World Convention officers— Charles Sanderson Medbury of the United States, William Morrow of Australia, and Harry H. Peters of the United States. As mentioned, the evening session featured messages from the youth.

There was no convention session Sunday morning to allow attendees to visit local churches. Sixty-two American preachers filled pulpits throughout England that day. In the afternoon was the World Convention communion service. Sunday evening's sermon was on "The Supremacy of Christ," followed by the Hallelujah Chorus sung by the Convention choir and a benediction from President John Wycliffe Black.

As in Washington, prayer and singing were a central part of the Convention. A prayer room was open throughout each day. A 400 member international choir was under the direction of Harrell Baird of Birmingham, Alabama. Attendees particularly remarked on the quality of the congregational singing.

Also, as in Washington, the Leicester Convention approved several resolutions concerning the moral and political issues of the day—race relations, peace and war, liquor and drugs, gambling, the economic situation, evangelism, education, and Christian unity. In light of events in Germany, Italy, and elsewhere, there was a strongly worded resolution condemning the totalitarian state and calling for freedom of conscience.

Before and after the Convention, there were twelve different tours throughout the British Isles and Europe open to attendees through the American Express Company. On the Monday after the Convention, almost all the attendees participated in an excursion to Stratford-upon-Avon.

The success of the Leicester Convention proved that a global gathering of the Stone-Campbell churches could be organized outside the numerical strength of the Movement in the United States. The program reflected the three lasting expressions of the purpose of World Convention—missions, unity, and fellowship.

.

Chapter
3

Postwar and Down Under: Buffalo and Melbourne

At the Leicester Convention, George H. Stewart of Canada was chosen as President with Toronto the designated site for the 1940 Convention. From 1935 to 1939, the Executive Committee and the Program Committee made preliminary plans, printed and distributed brochures to promote the Toronto meeting, and even had costs for transportation for those attending from Australia, New Zealand, and Britain. However, the outbreak of World War II, with Canada entering the war on September 10, 1939, caused the officers of the convention to indefinitely postpone the convention.

However, World Convention entered a new phase of its work in 1937. In that year, Jesse Bader attended both the Universal Christian Council for Life and Work Conference in Oxford, England, and the Second World Conference on Faith and Order in Edinburgh, Scotland as a representative of World Convention. From its beginning, World Convention's purposes have been to promote fellowship in the Stone-Campbell Movement and to work with all Christians toward the unity of the entire church. The 1937 Life and Work and Faith and Order meetings laid the groundwork for the formation of the World Council of Churches. In writing of the Life and Work meeting, Bader said, ". . . two things were most noticeable to me. One was the oft-repeated reference to Christian Unity and its utter necessity, and the other was the many references to the New Testament."[15]

During World War II, Bader held twenty-eight Chaplain's Conferences in Army and Navy bases throughout the United States. In 1938, 1939, and 1942, he preached on the nationwide NBC radio network. In 1940, he led the Federal Council of Churches to endorse World Communion Sunday, an ecumenical celebration followed by most Protestant Churches worldwide.

The Third Convention, Buffalo, New York, U.S.A., 1947

The postponement due to the war meant there were twelve years between Conventions. After the war, plans began again for the Convention to be held in Toronto in 1947 with George H. Stewart of Canada still President. However, the planners soon discovered a shortage of hotel rooms. The eighteen churches in the Buffalo, New York area (100 miles from Toronto) persuaded the executive committee to have the World Convention there, preceded by the International Convention (as had been the case in Washington). Stewart remained as President, making this Convention in many ways jointly hosted by Canadian and United States Disciples. Planning was done by a joint committee of 48 people representing the International and World Conventions.

The Convention opened on Sunday afternoon, August 3, at Memorial Auditorium in Buffalo, with a joint communion service with the International Convention, attended by over 15,000. That

---

[15] Letter from Jesse Bader to R.H. Miller, July 29, 1937

evening was the traditional parade of flags, with forty-two nations represented. This was the same number of nations present at Leicester twelve years earlier, reflecting the decline of international missions during the Great Depression. The opening address that night was by George Stewart.

1947 Buffalo crowd

Monday morning's session included reports on the churches in Great Britain, Central Europe, New Zealand, and Australia. This was followed by the All Nations Luncheon at which representatives from each of the other nations present made brief one minute reports. Monday afternoon the focus was on ecumenism, with Presbyterian Paul C. Payne speaking on behalf of the Sunday School Union, Congregationalist A.M. Chirgwin speaking on behalf of the International Missionary Council, Edwin McNeill Poteat, Jr., speaking on behalf of the Baptist World Alliance, and W.J. Gallagher of the United Church of Canada, speaking in behalf of the World Council of Churches. Gallaher's address is noteworthy since the World Council of Churches was still coming into being in 1947, a year before its first assembly at Amsterdam. Separate afternoon tea programs for youth and adults began on Monday and were held daily throughout the Convention. Methodist E. Stanley Jones, the best known missionary of the time, gave the address Monday evening, focusing on Christianity in India.

Christian education through the home, Sunday School, colleges and universities, and journalism was the theme Tuesday morning. The afternoon session featured a panel discussing the church and world peace. One highlight that afternoon was a musical presentation by the four Managbanag sisters from the Philippines. Tuesday evening's sessions were led by the youth with presentations on what youth are thinking and doing in various parts of the world.

Wednesday, August 6, began with a morning session devoted to the relationship between unity and evangelism, with William Robinson of England and P. H. Welshimer as two of the speakers. That afternoon the Convention held its business session, choosing Reginald Ennis of Australia as its next President and naming Melbourne as its next meeting place. Also in the afternoon, speakers from India, Australia, New Zealand and the United States spoke on "Human Relations in My Nation." The presentation by Cleo Blackburn, an African American Disciple leader from the United States, was significant for its honest account of race relations in that country. The most notable address at the Convention was given Wednesday night by Presbyterian layman John Foster Dulles,

United States Delegate to the United Nations, later to be Secretary of State under President Dwight Eisenhower. Entitled, "The Church's Opportunities in World Affairs," the speech called war "intolerable" and challenged the Convention attendees to use their moral power to achieve peace, calling the United Nations, "a place where the moral conscience of the world can drive the nations into following policies of justice, righteousness, and concord." Dulles's speech was covered widely by the newspapers.

EVERY CHRISTIAN A CRUSADER

Buffalo Platform

The last day of the Convention focused on World Evangelism. Morning and afternoon attendees heard speeches on evangelism in Mexico, Jamaica, South America, Puerto Rico, Japan, China, the Philippines, India, Siam (Thailand), Africa, and Central Europe. That evening the Convention ended with an address by Walter H. Judd, "The Present Necessity for World Missionary Conquest," followed by the Hallelujah Chorus and benediction.

The Buffalo Convention closely followed the structure of the Leicester Convention, including a "picnic" to Niagara Falls on the day following the Convention. However the number of speakers from outside the Stone-Campbell Movement made Buffalo notable. This Convention also made use of the latest technology with several motion picture films on world cultures being shown daily. As with previous World Conventions, the Buffalo meeting passed several resolutions on evangelism, Christian unity, the status of persons displaced by war, and those churches who were in "difficult areas" of the world. Of note is the resolution rejoicing in the formation of the Church of South India, and in the formation of the World Council of Churches.

After the third Convention, Jesse Bader was busy planning for the fourth, but also busy in wider ecumenical circles. As a fraternal delegate of the World Convention of Churches of Christ, he attended the inaugural Assembly of the World Council of Churches in Amsterdam, Netherlands, August 22 to September 4, 1948. He also attended the meetings of the Central Committee of the World Council in Chichester, England in 1949, in Toronto, Canada in 1950, and in Rolle, Switzerland in 1951.

The Fourth World Convention, Melbourne, Australia, 1952

In 1845 Thomas Magarey (1825–1902) and his family moved to Adelaide, South Australia from New Zealand. There they began the first Church of Christ in Australia in 1848. In New South Wales, the church began in 1851 through the work of William Stinson and John Hodges, immigrants from England. In 1853, the first church in Victoria was begun around Melbourne. The Victorian churches grew and multiplied due to evangelism so that by the mid-1860s there were twelve churches with a total of 230 members. At that time South Australia and New South Wales had three churches each.

As the congregations multiplied, cooperation meetings to promote evangelism were begun that grew into State Conferences in Victoria (1873), South Australia (1875), New South Wales (1885),

Western Australia (1898), Tasmania (1894) and Queensland (1901). In 1906 the First Federal Conference was held.

In 1907, the Australian churches began the College of the Bible in Melbourne, relocated to the suburb of Glen Iris in 1910 when A.R. Main (1876–1945) became its principal. This school continues to train leaders for the churches. The campus was moved to Mulgrave (another Melbourne suburb) in 1989 and renamed the Church of Christ Theological College, being renamed again in 2011 as Stirling College after longtime principal Gordon Stirling (1914–2010).

From 1914 to 1941, A.R. Main also served as editor of the official paper of the Federal Conference, the *Australian Christian.*

The Australian churches began foreign missions in the 1880s, forming the General Foreign Missions Committee in 1891. Missionaries were sent to the New Hebrides (now Vanuatu), India, Japan, and Africa. The General Foreign Missions Committee eventually became the current Global Mission Partners who work with churches in Bangladesh, India, Indonesia, Papua New Guinea, South Sudan, Thailand, Vanuatu, Vietnam and Zimbabwe.

The Australian churches have also been influential in ecumenical work, first under the leadership of A.R. Main and then T.H. Scambler (1879–1944) who became principal of the school at Glen Iris in 1938. The Federal Conference in 1946 affiliated with the Australian Committee for the World Council of Churches.

This brief history of the churches in Australia displays the theological and organizational maturity they had to hold a successful Convention in spite of postwar challenges. Planning for the Melbourne Convention hit a snag over the lack of cruise ships in the Pacific so soon after World War 2. Some thought was given to moving the location to Edinburgh, Scotland, but instead the Executive Committee of the Convention decided to postpone the Melbourne Convention until 1952. One challenge facing the

Executive Committee was the $2703 deficit[16] after the Buffalo Convention. Bader personally loaned money to defray those expenses and by July 1948 had raised money to lower the deficit to $484.

Melbourne platform

By 1952, the world economy saw great postwar improvement. This allowed 176 American and Canadians to attend the Australian Convention. Most went by ship through England, but 86 came to Australia on two chartered Pan American planes. Cost of those flights were $900 per person round trip ($8160 in 2017 dollars), a great expense at the time but still cheaper than the fares by ship. Those on the flight made a one day stop in Honolulu, where the First Christian Church hosted them at a traditional luau. Three around the world itineraries were also available with stops including Japan, the Philippines, Singapore, Thailand, India, Pakistan, Jerusalem, Egypt, Lebanon, Greece, Italy, France, and London.

Registrations for the Melbourne Conference were 3501, with attendees from ten countries. Although there were fewer countries

---

[16] Equals $29,119 in 2017

represented than at previous Conventions, this was a remarkable turnout in light of the difficulty of travel. The Melbourne
Convention was the first worldwide gathering of a Christian World
Communion to be held in Australia. Local, state, and national
Australian political leaders assisted in bringing the convention
to Melbourne, helping to secure Melbourne Town Hall with an
auditorium seating 2500 as the venue for the program.

The 71,721 members[17] of Australian Churches of Christ with the
leadership of Reg Innes and several others on committees organized a well-run and hospitable Convention. Melbourne was the
obvious city to host, with 73 Churches of Christ in the area, more
than any other city in the world at that time. On the Sunday before
the Convention opened, 80 preachers from outside Australia filled
pulpits in Melbourne.

The overall theme was "Our Christian Witness in a Confused
World," with Acts 1:8, "Ye shall be my witnesses . . . to the ends of
the earth" as the text. As with previous Conventions, the major
themes addressed were Christian unity, evangelism and mission,
and the church's response to global conditions. The Convention
opened Tuesday night, August 5, 1952 with the usual roll call of
nations and pageant of flags. Jesse Bader gave a brief history of
World Convention. Reg Ennis then gave the Presidential address
on "This Confused World and You," saying ". . . Christ's programme
for life is the solution of all the ills of individuals and nations. But
the church has so far failed to impress the world with its message
in any big way: men are not convinced that the church has or can
substantiate its claim."

The daily schedule was similar to that of previous Conventions,
with some notable new features. The reports on churches from each
nation were spread throughout the Convention schedule, with two

---

[17] According to the Australian religious census.

reports at each session. In addition to longer addresses, each day had at least one symposium on a topic with three to four speakers. Wednesday morning's theme was Evangelism with the symposium on "Effective Evangelism for Today." Another new feature was daily lunch hour programs on contemporary issues; the one Wednesday focused on "Christianity's Answer to Communism." The afternoon symposium was on Christian education, followed by the All Nations Tea at the Independent Church Hall next to the Town Hall. Alan Walker of Sydney, Australia gave the evening address on "The Church—A Living Witness."

Thursday morning focused on missions with a symposium on missionary methods. The lunch hour speech gave Jesus as the panacea for world unrest. Most significant was the afternoon session on "A Christian Women's World Fellowship." After four speakers shared on that theme at the symposium, Jessie Trout gave the primary address, calling for a World Christian Women's Fellowship that would promote connection among women in the Stone-Campbell movement worldwide but would also allow ecumenical fellowship with Christian women globally. This speech would lead to the formation at Toronto in 1955 of the World Christian Women's Fellowship, later known as Global Women Connecting, a sister organization to World Convention. A Missionary Tea preceded the evening session on Thursday that also highlighted world mission.

The Symposium on Friday morning was on "The Church and Human Relations," with presentations on race relations, world peace, and the church's responsibility for the dispossessed. At the World Convention business session that afternoon, a Constitution was adopted that called for an Executive Committee to transact the business of the World Convention between meetings, appoint committee members and officers, and plan the program. The rest of the afternoon and evening sessions dealt with Christian unity. However, unlike the Buffalo Convention, there were no speakers from outside the Stone-Campbell family. Also that evening, Earl Carlson presented the report on the churches in the United States, a report remarkable because it spoke solely of the Disciples of Christ with no mention of the Independents and their entities such as the North American Christian Convention. There was also no mention of the a cappella Churches of Christ. There were no speakers on the Melbourne program from the Independents or the a cappella churches. Indeed, for the next several decades almost all support and participation in World Convention from the United States would come from Disciples.

Saturday August 9 there were two significant events for attendees. First was the conference excursion or picnic by motorcoaches to the Dandenong mountains outside of Melbourne. That evening was the youth session featuring an original play, "Bread for the World," performed by the Victorian Churches of Christ Young People's Department, focusing on Jesus as the bread of life.

Convention attendees visited local churches on Sunday morning, August 10. The final Convention session was that night at the Exhibition Building in Melbourne attended by over 10,000. This was a dedication service, not a communion service since communion had been taken in local churches that morning. The Convention ended with the 300 member choir (led by Valentine Woff) presenting the Hallelujah Chorus, congregational singing of "God Be with You Till We Meet Again," an announcement of the next Convention in Toronto in 1955, and a benediction.

The Convention passed resolutions on evangelism, Christian unity, and one calling for a "such world order as will eventuate to the glory of God and the truest betterment of mankind. . . ." Other resolutions encouraged churches in India, Latin America, and all churches in difficult areas. Another resolution urged the democratic nations to open their doors to receive those displaced persons from the Second World War.

Reaction to the Melbourne Convention was overwhelmingly positive. Most agreed with Bader who said, "Of the four World Conventions since 1930, none was better prepared for or reached a higher peak of inspiration, instruction, fellowship, and spiritual power than the one held in Melbourne." As with all conventions, the personal relationships that were formed were the greatest blessing. Attendee S.A. Crouch wrote, "When I read of the work of the church in the New Hebrides, I say, 'I know Abel Barney, the native preacher of our work there, I met him at the Convention.' . . . When I read of the churches in Australia . . . there comes before me a vision of the ministers I met, the men of the churches, the women of the churches, the youth of the brotherhood. Because I met them I understand them better. Because I understand them better, I appreciate and love them more and more."[18] Many felt the same as ninety-one year old attendee I.N. McCash from the United States, who, when parting from the group in San Francisco, said, "I'll see you all at the next Convention in Toronto in 1955."

---

[18] S.A. Crouch, "The Fourth Convention of the Christian Church," *The Louisiana Christian* (October 1952), 4.

Organization and Study, Toronto and Edinburgh

1954 was a year of change for Jesse Bader and for World Convention. For over 24 years Bader led World Convention while working full time first as Superintendent of Evangelism for the United Christian Missionary Society in Indianapolis, Indiana, then as Executive Secretary of the Department of Evangelism for the Federal Council of Churches of Christ in America, based in New York City. However, in 1954, Bader resigned from the Federal Council and became full-time General Secretary of World Convention at a salary of $5000 per year.[19] This meant a move for the offices of World Convention to the Flatiron Building on 5th Avenue in New York, along with the adoption of an annual budget of $15,000.[20] The development of a Constitution and a paid General Secretary gave World Convention more organizational stability.

---

[19] $44,653 in 2017 dollars.
[20] $133,961 in 2017 dollars.

In 1954, Bader also attended the Second Assembly of the World Council of Churches in Evanston, Illinois.

1955—Edgar Gordon Burton and Jesse Bader

Fifth World Convention, Toronto, Canada, 1955

The short three year period between the Melbourne and Toronto Conventions required the Program and Arrangements Committee to meet five times in 1954 and three times in 1955. The Convention was an ambitious undertaking for the 80 congregations and 6500 members of the Disciple churches in Canada. The Hillcrest Church in Toronto with 434 members shouldered most of that load, with a planning committee and 17 subcommittees covering all the logistics of the Convention. President Edgar Gordon Burton, a layman and businessman, provided leadership and organizational skills. This was the first time that the World Convention had met apart from another convention, since national conventions had been held immediately previous to the Washington, Leicester, Buffalo, and Melbourne World Conventions.

Maple Leaf Gardens, a sporting arena seating 12,437, was the site for the Convention. The 7652 registered attendees were housed in over a dozen hotels, dormitories of the University of Toronto, Victoria College, and Knox College, and in private homes. The Hillcrest Church provided "overseas" guests with free housing and breakfast in the homes of church members. This was a generous gesture since there were 65 attendees from Australia, 40 from Great Britain, twelve from New Zealand, and over fifty from other countries outside North America. Registration fees were $3.50 each for those from North America, $1.50 each for others, and $1.50 for those under 14 years of age. Pre and post-convention tours could be booked from Indianapolis by bus, train, and steamship to Toronto and then to Montreal and Ottawa.

Advertised as a "family convention," this was the first to have an organized program for children under age fourteen. Housed at Shelbourne United Church, 437 children participated each day in a morning Vacation Bible School, lunch, and afternoon excursions to gardens, the zoo, art galleries, and museums. The program was led by a paid staff of 49 along with volunteers. The fee was $7.50 per child.

The other new feature of the Convention was a series of Study Breakfasts on Wednesday and Thursday. Two months after the Melbourne Convention resolution established a Study Committee, the committee of fourteen met and made plans to establish twenty-five study groups in fifteen countries, 210 scholars from all around the world, to prepare study guides for the breakfasts in Toronto. The 1873 people who purchased tickets for the Study Breakfasts were divided into eleven study groups, each discussing one of six topics—the nature of the church, the place of theology in the church, Christian baptism, the Lord's Supper, Christian ministry, and Christian hope. O.L. Shelton, Dean of the School of Religion at Butler University, was the chair of the Study Committee. Each of the study sessions was chaired by prominent scholars in the movement. Perhaps these sessions were an attempt to globalize similar studies made by the Commission on Restudy of the Disciples of Christ in North America from 1934–1949. The Toronto studies were published as a series of pamphlets and then in book form in 1956,[21] influencing the work of the Panel of Scholars of North American Disciples that worked from 1957–1962, some of whom had been chairs of the study sessions in Toronto.

Women were prominent at the Toronto Convention. The opening session on Tuesday, August 16, was a Christian Women's fellowship Luncheon at the Royal Oak Hotel, attended by 1485. Twelve women gave formal greetings from the women in their country, Lillian Thomson of Canada spoke on "The Role of Christian Women in the World Today," and Jesse M. Trout introduced plans for a World Christian Women's Fellowship.

That evening attendees saw the Convention theme, "Our Christian Commitment—A Christian World" emblazoned in large letters before a world map at the front of Maple Leaf Gardens. President Edgar Gordon Burton was presented with a gavel made of wood from the Cane Ridge Meeting House. The traditional pageant of the flags of the thirty-two countries where there were Stone-Campbell churches followed, with R.S. Garfield Todd, Prime Minister of Southern Rhodesia, carrying his country's flag. Burton then gave the presidential address, celebrating "the one and only organization that binds us all together . . . the World Convention, which came into being twenty-five years ago at Washington, D.C." He continued, "There is room within our World Convention fellowship for all brethren, no matter what differing opinions they may hold or what differing methods they may use in carrying out their work. The World Convention is an inclusive circle, large enough to include all our members within its fellowship."

---

[21] O.L. Shelton, *Doctrines of the Christian Faith* (St. Louis: Christian Board of Publication, 1956).

Wednesday began with the study breakfasts, followed by a morning plenary session on "A Christian World Through Individual Commitment." After presentations on the good confession that Jesus is the Christ, the entire audience was asked to reaffirm their confession and recommit their lives to

1955—Cleo Blackburn and R.S. Garfield Todd

Jesus Christ. Many called this the most moving experience of the Convention. Wednesday afternoon focused on Christian education through the home, church school, Christian literature, and Christian colleges. That evening the theme was Christian Witness, with R.S. Garfield Todd speaking on, "Our Timeless Missionary Mandate," where he tied the prayer of Jesus for unity with the command to teach all nations.

The Study Breakfasts on Thursday preceded a symposium on evangelism, with P.H. Welshimer and others calling for every Christian to be an evangelist. A. Dale Fiers spoke at the All Nations luncheon, with 1033 attendees. The afternoon session focused on Christian Missions. The first banquet for college students drew 441 to hear A.B.B. Moore, President of Victoria College of the University of Toronto. "A Christian World Through a Christian World Order" was the subject of the evening session, with two speakers from outside the Stone-Campbell Movement—O. Frederick Nolde, Associate General Secretary of the World Council of Churches, and Lester B. Pearson, Canadian Secretary of State, who later would win the Noble Prize for Peace and become Prime Minister of Canada.

Robert J. McCracken, successor to Harry Emerson Fosdick as minister at Riverside Church in New York was the speaker at the

Minister's Breakfast on Friday, August 19. The morning plenary symposium included an address by Cleo W. Blackburn, President of Jarvis Christian College that focused on racism. Every World Convention had passed a resolution condemning racism, but Blackburn challenged the delegates by saying, "Therefore we can do more than make general statements that we are against sin and we are against intolerance. The Church has the challenge of working out practical, down-to-earth, day-by-day programs within its institutions, within the church itself. . . ."

1955 marked twenty-five years of World Convention, celebrated at the Jubilee Luncheon on Friday, to which all attendees were invited. Citations of appreciation were given to Jesse Bader as General Secretary and to H. B. Holloway as Business Manager for their service since the inception of World Convention. Speaker Theo O. Fisher praised World Convention as ". . . a good instrument of God in leveling any fences of misunderstanding and difference. It has bridged the oceans, leaped over national boundaries, and called us from isolation, together in the name of Christ . . ."

Friday afternoon's session was an extended report by O.L. Shelton and James G. Clague on the work of the Study Committee and the Study Breakfasts. Stephen J. England, Dean of the College of the Bible at Phillips University, then gave an address placing those beliefs in the context of the ecumenical movement. Rejoicing that "For the first time in our history, we have self-consciously engaged in theological discussion," England said, "the documents of Toronto will make a genuine contribution to the Ecumenical Movement, and will bring us, as a people, more clearly into that Movement . . ." The theme of the evening session was Christian unity, with speaker C.G. Taylor of Australia asking, "What has happened to the passion with which this Movement was born?"

Saturday morning began with ten interest group breakfasts, including colleges, evangelistic organizations, and religious publishers. These groups also had exhibits in the convention. Then there were three concurrent morning sessions. The women's session was the first official meeting of the World Christian Women's Fellowship where Hilda Green of England was elected President, and Jessie Trout as Secretary-Treasurer. $1004 was given in contributions for the new organization. A men's session featured reports on men's work from various countries. Paul Crow, later to be President of the Council on Christian Unity, presided at the youth session that included a panel discussion on youth work on five continents. Saturday afternoon over two thousand of the attendees boarded fifty-nine buses for a tour of Toronto. That night a panel of youth discussed, "A Christian World Through Youth Committed to Christ." This was followed by the Hallelujah Chorus and the Lord's Prayer.

The greatest ecumenical experience of the Convention was attending Anglican, Baptist, Presbyterian, and United Church of Canada worship services throughout Toronto. There eighty-one Disciple ministers filled pulpits. A Sunday afternoon service at the Hillcrest Church of Christ was broadcast live on radio by the Canadian Broadcasting Corporation. The Convention ended with a 3:30 communion service attended by over 5000.

The Resolutions Committee proposed and the Convention passed twelve resolutions, three on the central concerns of World Convention—Christian unity, missions, and education—and nine dealing with global concerns like war, poverty, race relations, and relief for refugees.

Many considered the Toronto Convention the best held in the twenty-five years. As Bader reported in the *Christian-Evangelist*, "Above and beyond all that happened was this: Christ, in whose name we came together, was among us and his spirit and power were felt by the World Convention delegates."[22]

The Sixth World Convention, Edinburgh, Scotland, 1960

Charles K. Green, President, from Manchester, England worked with the Executive Committee of thirty-one persons from fifteen countries in planning the program for Edinburgh. R.S. Garfield Todd, Dean Walker, and David Lloyd Sanders were notable members of the Executive Committee. As at Toronto, the local work largely fell on a single congregation, the two hundred member Dalkeith Road Church of Christ in Edinburgh, assisted by the churches in Great Britain.

Jesse Bader was busy not only with preparation for Edinburgh but with the worldwide ecumenical activities of World Convention. He attended the meetings of the Central Committee of the World Council of Churches in Budapest, Hungary in 1956, New Haven, Connecticut in 1957, and St. Andrews, Scotland in 1960. He was also at the inaugural annual meeting of the Secretaries of Christian World Communions at Yale University in 1957. He attended world gatherings of the Lutheran World Federation, the International Congregational Council, and the World Methodist Council. Typical of his travel schedule to Stone-Campbell churches, in 1958 he visited churches in 20 countries in 18 weeks, covering 45,000 miles. Bethany Press also published his book, *Evangelism in a Changing America* in 1957. He also found time in 1957 to lead the local evangelism crusade following the Billy Graham Crusade in New York. World Convention took another ecumenical step in 1960 by appointing Hugh D. Darsie as its observer to the United

---

[22] Jesse M. Bader, "It Happened at Toronto!" *Christian-Evangelist* (September 15, 1955), 19.

Nations in New York. Fraternal delegates were also sent to the Lausanne Youth Meeting, the World Christian Student Federation, and the World Council of Christian Education.

1960 was a momentous year for the city of Edinburgh, marking the 400th anniversary of the Scottish Reformation and the 50th anniversary of the World Missionary Conference that was the beginning of the modern ecumenical movement. The Edinburgh World Convention marked the anniversaries with its theme, "The Church Committed to Christ—Concerned for Man." As attendees entered Usher Hall for the Convention, they marveled at an impressive eight feet by twelve feet mural, commissioned by the World Christian Women's Fellowship and designed by Mrs. Barton Johnson of Covington, Kentucky, USA. The mural, entitled "Come Unto Me," pictured Jesus centered between the two global hemispheres which were surrounded by handicrafts representing the twenty-three countries where the World CWF was doing mission work. The mural was manufactured by the Formica Company using the techniques of artlay, inlay, and hand-painting.

Plane on the way to 1960 Convention

The pageant of flags opened the Convention on the evening of Tuesday, August 2, 1960. J.H.S. Burleigh, Moderator of the General Assembly of the Church of Scotland brought fraternal greetings. This was followed by the reading of a resolution celebrating the 400th Anniversary of the Scottish Reformation. For the first time, a World Convention had no resolutions on the world situation. A gavel made from wood from a house church in Wales where Alexander Campbell had preached was presented to President Charles K. Green. Green then gave the presidential address on the subject of stewardship. Over 4000 registrants from thirty-three countries were in attendance, an overflow crowd hearing the address through loudspeakers in the nearby Lothian Road Church of Scotland (St. Cuthbert's Church).

The theme for Wednesday, August 3 was "The Message and Mission of the Church." The morning began with a report on the churches in the Philippines. These national reports were spread throughout the sessions of the Convention, under the heading of "Christ at Work Among My People." This was followed by an international panel on "Communicating the Christian Message." The panel and subsequent message by Gordon Stirling of Australia made it clear that the mission of the church was a broad one. In Stirling's words, "Not only is the Church charged with the task of reconciling men to God. She is charged with the task of reconciling to God industry, commerce, economics, politics, and international relations." In the afternoon was a missionary rally, honoring missionaries and national workers from many countries. One new feature of the Edinburgh Convention was the offering of interest group dinners focused on enhancing the work of congregations. That evening's speaker was Perry Gresham, President of Bethany College, who spoke on the influence of Scotland on the thought of Alexander Campbell.

"The Faith and Fellowship of the Church" was Thursday's topic. Jean Bokeleale of the Congo spoke on "The Dimensions of Christian Fellowship." The two luncheons that day were for the World Christian Women's Fellowship and for Ministers. That afternoon and Friday afternoon, attendees had the choice of twelve study groups (as in Toronto), on one of six topics: The Nature of the Unity We Seek, The Congregation and the Body of Christ, Who is Jesus Christ, the Authority in Religion, the Theology of Evangelism, and Ethical Demands of the Gospels. In the five years prior to Edinburgh, twenty-two members of the Study Committee had gathered thirty-four groups in nineteen countries

1960—Edinburgh crowd

to prepare study materials. The results of the Edinburgh studies were later published.[23] That evening, World Convention citations honored Cynthia Pearl Maus of the United States, R.S. Garfield

---

[23] *Doctrines of the Christian Faith* (St Louis: Christian Board of Publication, 1961).

Todd of Southern Rhodesia (Zimbabwe), and William Robinson of the United Kingdom for their service to the Stone-Campbell Movement. Lesslie Newbigin, Bishop of the Church of South India, also received a citation for his leadership in global missions.

Thursday evening's speaker was from outside the Stone-Campbell family. George F. MacLeod was a Church of Scotland minister and the founder of the Iona Community. Beginning his address by saying, "God became Man that Man might become God," MacLeod later said, "Man has a simple choice before him—to blow himself up or to take off for the stars. Only the church has the key to the affluent society or to any other. That key is the church's concern for the whole man."

Two particularly eloquent addresses marked Friday's program. In the morning Stephen J. England spoke on "The Church—Her Historical Destiny." Although he characterized our historical period as "post-Christian," he added, "I should like, however, to risk characterizing our days as a time not only of spiritual poverty but also of spiritual hunger." The All Nations Luncheon followed the morning session. That evening, in his address on "The Church Knows No Boundaries," R.S. Garfield Todd stated, "When I speak of the Church breaking boundaries and concerning herself with the affairs of the world, I am not visualizing the Church as a great machine, organized on an authoritarian basis, wielding power upon earth through force and intrigue. I have in my mind the concept of an ideal Church, of congregations of humble men and women, deeply concerned for their fellows, and ready at any cost to themselves to serve effectively so the leaven of the love of God may permeate every situation."

The World Christian Women's Fellowship, Men's Christian Fellowship, and Christian Youth Fellowship each met in separate simultaneous sessions on Saturday morning. The youth, ages 15–28, had met in separate sessions throughout the Convention at

Middleton Residential School Camp outside of Edinburgh. That afternoon was the Convention sightseeing tour of Edinburgh in city buses. The evening session was led by the youth with the theme of total commitment to Christ.

Sunday morning Convention goers attended local church services, primarily in Church of Scotland congregations. Because of the size of the crowd, two simultaneous communion services were held in the afternoon at Usher Hall and at the Lothian Road Church of Scotland. The Convention ended that evening in Usher Hall with A. Dale Fiers speaking on "Lighten Our Darkness." For the first time in its history the Convention ended not with the Hallelujah Chorus but with the hymn, "In Christ There is No East or West."

Arthur N. Wake of the College of the Bible in Lexington, Kentucky directed the 334 voice Convention choir. Worship at Edinburgh was more liturgical that at previous Conventions, with printed responsive readings and prayers in the program book. Although the fifty-eight speakers on the program were from many nations and included ecumenical speakers from outside the Stone-Campbell churches, an article by Hugh F. Sensibaugh in the *Christian Standard* said Theo O. Fisher, the chair of the Program Committee, admitted that no attempt was made to include speakers who were not connected to the International Convention. Sensibaugh adds that Jesse Bader, however, showed an attitude of inclusive fellowship.[24]

In addition to the *Christian Standard*, there was extensive coverage of the Convention in *The Christian* (USA), the *Australian Christian*, the *Disciple* (Canada), the *New Zealand Christian*, and many other state, regional, and national papers of the Stone-Campbell Movement. Local reporting in the Edinburgh

---

[24] Hugh F. Sensibaugh, "Impressions of a Conventiongoer," (*Christian Standard*, October 8, 1960), 7.

papers was glowing with praise for the organization and spirit of the Convention.

The most extensive offerings of pre and post-Convention tours were made in association with American Express. World Convention made enough from the tours to begin an endowment for its continuing work. In the year preceding Edinburgh, World Convention had maintained offices in New York and Indianapolis, spending a total of $40,912 ($337,750 in 2017 dollars). An average yearly budget of $36,000 for each of the next five years was proposed. Income was solely from donations from individuals and congregations, and from registration and tour fees from the Conventions. Thus the need for an endowment.

Ecumenism and Restructure: Vatican II and San Juan

Immediately after the Edinburgh Convention, planning began for the 1965 Convention in San Juan, Puerto Rico, led by President Florentino Santana, minister for the Comerio Christian Church in Bayamon. However, Jesse Bader and others were also heavily involved in some of the most significant ecumenical work of the World Convention during the first years of the 1960's.

Vatican II

Bader and over forty other members of Stone-Campbell churches worldwide attended the third Assembly of the World Council of Churches in New Delhi, India, November 19 through December 5, 1961. World Convention sponsored a luncheon for attendees from those churches on November 21, with churches from Australia, Canada, Great Britain, New Zealand, Switzerland, the United States, India, and Puerto Rico present.

Jesse Bader at Vatican II

At the Secretaries of Christian World Communions meeting in Geneva, Switzerland, April 3–4, 1962, Augustin Cardinal Bea invited all the Christian Communions, including World Convention, to send official observers to the Second Vatican Council. The World Convention Executive Committee selected Jesse Bader as their observer. Thus it was that he, along with twenty-seven other Delegate Observers from fifteen world confessional bodies, witnessed the opening of the Vatican Council at St. Peter's Basilica, October 11, 1962.

Bader was present at all of the solemn (public) sessions and the closed General Assemblies of the first session of the Council. He took careful notes and made brief written reports back to the World Convention office. In reporting on the opening message of Pope John XXIII, Bader remarked, "There was not much in it that indicated that the Roman Catholic Church would make any radical change or reforms." Before the council was over, Bader and the other Protestant observers would indeed be surprised at the changes proposed.

Writing on October 18, Bader gave two impressions. One was that the council would likely make "a definite contribution to Christendom." The second was that "there is a noticeable change in attitude toward Protestants, Anglicans, and Orthodox Churches on the part of many of the leaders of the Roman Catholic Church, beginning with the current Pope." In his October 27 report, Bader was struck by the complete absence of women in the Council, saying "How different it is in most of our Protestant churches around the world in their assemblies." He remarked on the increased use of the Bible among Catholics in a latter report. His last report focused on the emphasis on Christian unity at the Council, particularly the work of Augustin Cardinal Bea and the Secretariat for Promoting Christian Unity. Bader concluded his reports by saying, "It has been a genuine privilege to represent the World Convention of Churches of Christ (Disciples) at the Second Vatican Council. I have been in Rome six weeks in attendance at this Council meeting. I have not missed a single session. During these six weeks I have been able to explain to many of the "fathers" of the Council and also to many of the delegate-observers, who we are, what we believe and our historic concern for Christian Unity."[25]

A significant internal change at World Convention was the appointment of Laurence V. Kirkpatrick as Associate General Secretary as of February 1, 1963. Kirkpatrick had served churches in Oklahoma, Ohio, and Kansas. He held a B.D. from Yale and a Ph.D. from Union Theological Seminary. From 1961 to 1963, he was on the staff of the World Council of Christian Education in

---

[25] For more on Bader and the Second Vatican Council, see Nadia Lahutsky, "We Owe it to Our Future: Disciples and Vatican II," *Disciples History* 73:2 (Fall 2014), 8–11, 20–23.

New York City. The plan was for Kirkpatrick to apprentice under Bader and to eventually become General Secretary.

That day came sooner than expected when Jesse Bader died on August 19, 1963, one week after suffering a stroke. Condolences came into the World Convention offices from Christian leaders throughout the world. For all thirty-three years of the World Convention, his vision, energy, and spirit had been its guiding force.

Larry Kirkpatrick stepped in immediately as acting General Secretary. In addition to the planning for the Puerto Rico Convention, he was an Observer at the Second Session of the Vatican Council in 1963, along with William G. Baker of Scotland. Baker, W.B. Blakemore, and Howard Short of the United States were observers during the Third Session in 1964. Blakemore was joined by Basil Holt of South Africa for the final Session in 1965.

A World Consultation on the Future of World Convention

One of the most significant meetings in the life of World Convention took place August 7–9, 1965 in Puerto Rico, preceding the Convention there. This World Consultation was an informal meeting of thirty-two national leaders from eleven countries. The purpose of the Consultation was to review the impact of the World Convention and its future activity in light of circumstances radically different from those in which the World Convention was born thirty-five years earlier.

This meeting on the purposes and future of World Convention was prompted primarily by tensions within the Disciples in North America who were in the process of changing their church structures. In 1961 the Commission on Brotherhood Restructure began its work, presenting a Provisional Design for the Christian Church (Disciples of Christ) to congregations, regions, and church agencies in 1966. After two years of study and response, the Provisional

Design was accepted at the Kansas City Convention in 1968. The result was a structure based on covenant that recognized three manifestations of church—congregational, regional, and general. The structures of the church were intended to be biblical, comprehensive, interrelated, ecumenical, and faithful, expressing both unity and diversity. One purpose of restructure was to make the church more effective in its mission of reconciliation.

However, Restructure caused some American Disciples to question the need for World Convention. They felt a more official national structure would allow American Disciples to join with other national bodies of Disciple churches in the United Kingdom, Australia, New Zealand, and eventually other nations to have a stronger ecumenical presence. The hope was for officially recognized dialogue with other denominations perhaps even leading to merger and union. In that context, they saw World Convention as a competing organization that was an unofficial mass meeting and not a representative of national churches. Leaders such as George G. Beazley, president of the Council on Christian Unity, believed continued Disciple support of World Convention would diffuse and undercut Disciple ecumenical efforts. This was part of a larger discussion in the Christian world as to whether confessionalism undercut ecumenism.

Tied to this concern was the reality of a second division in the Stone-Campbell Movement in the United States that affected churches worldwide. The tensions between cooperatives and independents among Disciples intensified during the 1930's to 1960's, the period of restudy and restructure of the Disciples. Between 1967 and 1972 about 750,000 adherents and 3500 congregations formally withdrew from the Disciples and formed the Christian Churches and Churches of Christ. Some congregations use Christian Church in their name, others Church of Christ (not to be confused with the earlier division that resulted in a cappella Churches of Christ). The plural "Churches" is significant since this group is organized congregationally with no official structure beyond the congregation.

From its inception, World Convention sought to serve all manifestations of the Stone-Campbell Movement. However, the leadership and funding for World Convention had come almost entirely from American Disciples. Some Disciples therefore saw no need to continue to support an organization that included some theologically opposed to their structure and their ecumenical efforts.

However, many influential American Disciples were very much in favor of continuing World Convention. During 1965, the International Convention of the Disciples in the United States and World Convention had formed a joint committee to discuss the relationship of the two organizations, including promotion and finance. It was in this context that the World Consultation met in Puerto Rico. Over three days, this informal discussion concluded that World Convention should continue to welcome the Independent Christian Churches and the a cappella Churches of Christ worldwide to the extent they wished to be included. They reflected on the variety of expressions of church in the Stone-Campbell Movement globally, with some of those churches organized nationally in various ways and some strictly congregational. They discussed financing with the New Zealand and Australian churches giving to World Convention through their national organizations while congregations and individuals gave in the United States and other countries. There was strong support, particularly from the United States Disciples, for including World Convention in the Unified Promotion of the International Convention, later called the Disciples Mission Fund of the Christian Church (Disciples of Christ).

One important distinction was made between the two aspects of the Convention, the Assemblies every five years and the ongoing work of the Convention office in promoting global unity in the

Stone-Campbell Movement and in ecumenical work, such as appointing observers to the Vatican II Council. The final statement of their report was "The members of the Consultation were unanimous in their feeling that the World Convention is a valuable and integral part of our World Fellowship."

Influential American Disciples, such as A. Dale Fiers who would become the first General Minister and President of the Christian Church (Disciples of Christ) were part of the Consultation. The Consultation helped clarify several matters regarding the relationship of World Convention to the Christian Church (Disciples of Christ). More mutual understanding came from a Liaison Committee between the World Convention and the Christian Church (Disciples of Christ) that met from 1969 to 1978, but tensions would remain, particularly with the Council on Christian Unity, for decades to come.

1965—Florentino Santana, Lawrence Kirkpatrick, and Michael Saenz

The Seventh World Convention, San Juan, Puerto Rico, 1965

In terms of location, attendance, language, and the variety and notoriety of speakers, the assembly in San Juan was a turning point for World Convention. The Stone-Campbell Movement had come to Puerto Rico early in the twentieth century soon after it became a possession of the United States. Nine denominational mission boards, including the United Christian Missionary Society of the Disciples, entered into a comity agreement, with Disciples being assigned the area around San Juan and Bayamon. By 1965, there were fifty seven congregations on the island with 8656 members.

1965—Platform at San Juan

Under the leadership of President Florentino Santana, minister for the Comerio Christian Church in Bayamon, and with the assistance of Laurence Kirkpatrick as acting General Secretary, the Puerto Rican Christians formed twenty-one committees to organize the Convention. Kirkpatrick and others worked hard to get Americans to come to Puerto Rico, emphasizing the affordability of the trip, with flight and housing costing only $185 to $250.[26]There were also 35 attendees from New Zealand, 29 from Australia, and at least 10 from the United Kingdom. Twenty-seven countries in all were represented. In light of the impending division among American Disciples, it is noteworthy that over fifty of the Independents were there, including well known leaders such as Robert O. Fife, Edwin V. Hayden, Hugh F. Sensibaugh, and Earl Stuckenbruck, on the program.

The Convention began on Monday evening, August 9, 1965 at the three year old Hiram Bithorn baseball stadium, seating 18,000. The 7500 attendees entering the stadium saw a banner

---

[26] $1410 to $1906 in 2017 dollars.

over the rostrum displaying the Convention Theme: "Jesu Cristo Es El Senor, Jesus Christ is Lord." This would be the first World Convention in two languages, Spanish and English, and that experience brought home to many attendees that the Stone-Campbell Movement had truly become global. After welcoming messages from the major of San Juan and the governor of Puerto Rico, President Santana gave the opening address on the Convention theme. Among other things, he reminded the crowd that "Christ is the Lord of rest and of the Sabbath. That means our rest, like our reflection and our meditation, has a precious place in his kingdom, certain and peaceful."

Because there was no enclosed auditorium large enough to seat the attendees, morning sessions were held in two venues simultaneously (much like the first Convention in Washington). Thus on Tuesday, August 10, J. Daniel Joyce spoke on "The Authority of the Bible" at a ballroom in El San Juan Hotel while K.J. Clinton spoke on the same theme at the San Jeronimo Hilton. Mae Yoho Ward then gave a moving address, first to one then to the second venue, on "Our Task in Witness," saying, "Surely no one has made his way to a *world* convention who is not convinced that the redemption of the world is our primary task . . ." Next Charles K. Green and Carl Ketcherside gave sermons at each of the venues. Ketcherside was the first World Convention speaker from a cappella Churches of Christ. His personal story reflected a change in those churches that would develop in the next few decades, a move from a narrow sectarianism to working toward unity among all the streams of the Stone-Campbell Movement. Quite conservative in his view of the Bible, it is remarkable that he said in his sermon, "The Christian concept is not one of Jesus pointing to a book but of a book pointing to Jesus."

Tuesday evening at Bithorn Stadium, there was an extensive session in memory of Jesse Bader. W.B. Blakemore remarked, "In

1930, he led in the establishment of this World Convention. . . . Bonds were kept which but for him and the Convention he represented might have been severed. His journeys wove the powerful pattern of Christian fellowship which is the center of our Assembly tonight." The memorial service was followed by a sermon by Basil Holt of South Africa on "The Mission of the Church in the World Today."

The practice of study breakfasts continued in San Juan. In the years preceding, fifty-eight study groups with over 900 individuals in fifteen countries had prepared material on ecumenism, worship, the Holy Spirit, the church, ministry, and biblical authority. That material was discussed by small groups at breakfast on Wednesday, Thursday, and Friday of the Convention, and later published in book form. After breakfast, the morning session focused on the church, with Ray Blampied and Philip Morgan leading Bible studies. This was followed by a symposium entitled, "God Calls His Church to Renewal." W.B. Blakemore spoke of Roman Catholic renewal, reporting on his experience as a delegate observer at Vatican II. Howard E. Short and Robert O. Fife spoke of Protestant renewal. Stephen J. England discussed the different views of renewal and restoration among Churches of Christ worldwide. Emmett Dickson and George R. Davis gave sermons on the church. The World Christian Women's Fellowship lunch and the Men's Fellowship lunch followed.

Wednesday evening began with the election of Laurence Kirkpatrick as the second General Secretary of World Convention. He had been working for years first as Associate, then as Acting Secretary after Bader's death. Over 7000 were present that night to hear one of the most notable speakers in World Convention history. Martin Niemoller was a Lutheran pastor, a leader of the Confessional church in Germany under Hitler, and a prisoner for eight years in the Sachsenhausen and Dachau concentration camps. After the war, he was a prominent leader in the ecumenical movement, and was one of the presidents of the World Council of Churches when he spoke in San Juan. In his sermon on "The Unity of the Church," he said, "Christian Friends! The unity of the church is not an aim, which we ought to accomplish by organizational union nor by

Florentino Santana and Martin Luther King

doctrinal adjustments. All this may be in vain, if we shall not—at first and basically—recognize Jesus the Christ as being the only one whom we are called to trust and follow, and who is our peace and communion."

The Christian Life was the theme on Thursday, August 12, with Bible studies followed by a symposium on "Christ's Impact on My World," with speakers from Africa, Asia, Australasia, Europe, Latin America, and North America. Martin Niemoller spoke again at the Ministers Luncheon while Golda Bader spoke at the Ministers' Wives Luncheon. Thursday evening was the Youth emphasis session where speaker Richmond Nelson of Jamaica prophetically challenged both young and old, "The Christian youth of this age cannot effectively serve Christ if they are only prepared to adjust themselves to the 'status quo.' . . .Therefore, there are certain ills in our Society to which we ought never to be adjusted. We must never adjust ourselves to religious bigotry. We must never adjust ourselves to any kind of oppression. We must never adjust ourselves to any kind of oppression, social and economic injustice. We must never adjust ourselves to racial segregation. We must never adjust ourselves to an ever widening gap between the 'haves' and the 'have-nots' in our Society."

Earl Stuckenbruck and T.J. Liggett led Bible studies Friday morning, followed by another sermon by Martin Niemoller. Carlos J. Lastra, the Secretary of State of Puerto Rico, then gave an address on "The Christian Community," where he spoke of serving Christ in the church community and the secular world. Friday night was an ecumenical night with a greeting and address from Luis Aponte Martinez, the Roman Catholic Archbishop of San Juan, followed by a sermon, "Jesus Christ is Lord Today," by Alfonso Rodriquez.

There were three simultaneous sessions Saturday morning— the World Christian Women's Fellowship, the Men's Fellowship, and the Youth Fellowship—followed by the All Nations Luncheon. Saturday evening, the largest crowd of any World Convention session, over 10,000, heard Martin Luther King, Jr. speak. The Puerto Rican Christians had asked for two American guests to speak at the Convention, Billy Graham and Martin Luther King. Graham was not able to commit to speaking because of health difficulties. King committed nine weeks before the Convention, thanks in part to the friendship between Laurence Kirkpatrick and Andrew Young, King's associate. King had received the Nobel Peace Prize just the previous year, and was well known and appreciated throughout Puerto Rico. Upon his arrival over one hundred local political leaders gave a breakfast for him in San Juan. No recording or manuscript of King's address to the Convention exists, but from the title, "A Christian Movement in a Revolutionary Age," it appears this was a speech he gave often in various locations in 1965.[27]

Sunday morning, August 15, Convention goers were encouraged to worship in local churches. At 7 p.m. there was a closing Communion Service where A. Dale Fiers called for discerning the body of Christ as the church in the world. "It was for the noble and

---

[27] For a manuscript of that speech see http://www.thekingcenter.org/archive /document/christian-movement-revolutionary-age

divine purpose of uniting and renewing the church according to the scriptures that our own movement came into being on the frontier of the new world. It is interesting to recall that the concerns that gave us birth as an identifiable part of the Church Universal centered around the Lord's table and the unity of the Body of Christ." After Fier's address, a new practice was begun of giving attendees souvenir communion cups, locally handmade miniatures with a multi-colored glaze.

As at other World Conventions, citations were given. Jesse Bader (posthumously), Charles Clayton Morrison (editor of the *Christian Century*), Stephen J. England, President Lyndon B. Johnson (a member of National City Christian Church in Washington), and Martin Niemoller were honored. President Johnson was presented with his citation at the White House.

Resolutions gave thanks for the life of Jesse Bader, and for the hospitality of the churches of Puerto Rico. There were also resolutions supporting ecumenism and calling for peace and for racial and economic harmony.

A large selection of pre and post-Convention tours took travelers throughout South America and the Caribbean. In addition, there were daily afternoon tours of Puerto Rico during the Convention.

In spite of the challenges of two languages and nightly rain at the stadium, the San Juan Convention was in many ways the most outstanding one yet. It had the greatest attendance, the most days, the widest variety of speakers, and the most notable presenters of any Convention.

Transition and Challenges: Adelaide and Mexico City

After the Puerto Rico Convention, World Convention continued its daily work of connecting Stone-Campbell churches worldwide and its work in the wider ecumenical movement. Much of that work between 1966 and 1974 was done through a Committee on World Interfaith Relations with W.B. Blakemore as chair. The committee, that eventually had twenty-seven members from nine countries, grew out of the experiences of Blakemore and others as Observers at Vatican II. Meeting annually, the committee promoted unity among all Christians, explored ways to have dialogue with Roman Catholics, and urged relations with Judaism and other religions. This work led to the Adelaide Convention's emphasis on ecumenism. In addition to the work of the committee, Larry Kirkpatrick attended the annual meetings of the Secretaries of Christian World Communions, the meeting of the Central Committee of the World Council of Churches in Heraklion, Crete in 1967, as well as the Fourth Assembly of the World Council of Churches in Uppsala, Sweden in 1968.

1970—Lawrence Kirkpatrick and Quantas representative

After many years of discussion with American Disciples, one important change in the way World Convention was funded took place in 1968 when it entered the Unified Promotion arrangement with the International Convention (soon to be the Christian Church (Disciples of Christ). Up to this time, World Convention had received annual gifts from individual Disciple congregations and from Disciple State Associations, for example, a total of $29,576 in 1967 (equals $212,731 in 2017 dollars). Now they would no longer solicit or receive direct gifts from those sources but those donations would go to Unified Promotion, the cooperative fundraising and distribution agency of the Disciples, who would allot an amount annually to World Convention. That amount was $28,495 in 1968. World Convention continues to receive an annual allotment from what is now called the Disciples Mission Fund.

The Eighth Assembly, Adelaide, South Australia, October 20–25, 1970

The Australian committee began work on the Adelaide Convention even before the Puerto Rico meeting ended. Although it had been eighteen years since the Convention in Melbourne, the lessons learned there about program and structure helped make the Adelaide Convention the most organized yet, with 26 local committees.

As at Melbourne, the Federal Conference of Australia and the World Convention were back-to-back in the same city. Also preceding the World Convention were two global meetings, a "World Brotherhood Consultation on Overseas Missions," with Jean B. Bokeleale of the Congo as a speaker, and a second World Consultation on the Work of the World Convention.

The Convention itself opened on Tuesday evening October 20 with the traditional pageant of flags from thirty-four nations. Over 6000 people from twenty-four countries jammed the newly opened Apollo Stadium for the opening, which was televised on the Australian Broadcasting Network. President Philip Messent gave a spiritual challenge to the attendees as a laymen and physician, not a trained theologian. Raymond McAllister spoke on the Convention theme, "One Gospel, One World," urging listeners to . . ."shift from noisy confusion to the composure of the contemplative life" and to move from mere church membership to discipleship. The crowd then sang a hymn written by T.J. Meade on the Convention theme.

As in the previous few Conventions, there were study breakfasts with 53 groups at various locations on Wednesday, Thursday, and Friday. The main morning sessions were at Centennial Hall in Wayville. Wednesday morning speakers from New Zealand, England, and Puerto Rico led a symposium on "The Christ of the Gospel." Douglas A. Dickey of the American Christian Churches gave the sermon, "Christ Defies Despair." The World Christian

Women's Fellowship Luncheon featured Rathie Salvaratnam as speaker. One new feature at Adelaide was a series of three addresses in the Adelaide Town Hall and open to the public by Philip Potter of Jamaica, later to be the third General Secretary of the World Council of Churches, as the inaugural Jesse M. Bader Lectureship on Contemporary Evangelism. Many attendees felt the highlight of the Convention was hearing Kosuke Koyama, Dean of the Southeast Asia School of Theology, preach on Wednesday night. Koyama spoke of the divine "slowness" of God who took the patient and painful way of the cross to save humanity.[28]

Joy Roberts at World Convention information booth

Thursday morning, October 22 began with two concurrent sessions, the World Christian Women's Fellowship and the Men's Session. That evening was the youth emphasis session, which included a dramatic presentation by the youth from Michael Quoist's *Prayers of Life*[29].

Friday's theme was "A World in Need," with a morning symposium with speakers from Latin America, Asia, and Africa. That evening World Convention presented citations to Jean B. Bokeleale, Edith Green, William Barnett Blakemore, Jr., Cleo W. Blackburn, and E. Lyall Williams. Garfield Todd had the evening sermon.

---

[28] He elaborates on this theme in his later books, *Waterbuffalo Theology* (Maryknoll, N.Y.: Orbis, 1974) and *Three Mile an Hour God* (London: SCM, 1979).

[29] Dublin: Gill and Macmillan, 1965.

Saturday morning began with a Ministers' Breakfast with James M. Moudy as speaker, followed by the business session where Larry Kirkpatrick shocked the crowd by announcing his resignation as General Secretary, effective July 1, 1971. His stated reason was a conviction that those who serve as leaders in the areas of the general work of the church should so serve for a limited period of time. The morning also featured a symposium on authority, sacraments, and ministry with Dean E. Walker as one of the presenters. That afternoon was a Garden Party for all attendees. That night was an ecumenical service planned by the Australian Council of Churches. The Adelaide Convention was by far the most ecumenical assembly of World Convention, in terms of speakers from outside the Stone-Campbell Movement.

Attendees were encouraged to visit local churches Sunday morning. The closing session Communion Service was that night, with the traditional singing of the Hallelujah Chorus. For the first time, there were no resolutions passed at the assembly.

1974 Allan Lee

Two significant events followed the Convention. On October 26–27, there was an International Ministers' Seminar with Kosuke Koyama as the primary presenter. From October 29 to November 1, there were Evangelistic Crusades in many of the Australian congregations, with Convention goers from all parts of the world as guest preachers.

Conventioneers could choose from a dozen tours before and after the assembly, ranging from 24 to 47 days in length and covering the South Pacific, Asia, the Holy Land, and Europe.

Press coverage of the Adelaide Convention was uniformly glowing both from secular and religious papers. Significant were the three very positive articles in the *Christian Chronicle*,[30] the best known newspaper among American a cappella Churches of Christ in the United States, since this was the first publicity about World Convention among that group.

Allan W. Lee, Third Secretary General

After serving as pastor at First Christian Church in Seattle, Washington, for almost twelve years, Allen Lee accepted the invitation to become General Secretary, effective September 1, 1971. Lee was no stranger to World Convention, having attended four assemblies, including Adelaide which inspired his brief book, *Disciple Down Under: A South Pacific Journey*.[31] Two summers working in Mexico with the Mexican Bible Society and Union Theological Seminary in Mexico City provided invaluable experience to aid in planning the 1974 Convention.

In the years preceding the Mexico City assembly, Lee not only had to quickly orient himself to his new position with much time in travel among the Stone-Campbell churches and ecumenically, but he also overcame two serious surgeries in his first year. He attended the Central Committee Meeting of the World Council of Churches in Utrecht, Netherlands, the annual meeting of the Secretaries of

---

[30] Vol. XXIII, November 9, 16, and 23, 1970.
[31] New York: Exposition Press, 1971.

World Christian Communions, and also had a private audience with Pope Paul VI in 1972. Lee began the first regular published news sheet of World Convention, *The World Conventioner,* in 1972. Much of his time in 1973 was spent in moving the World Convention Offices from New York City to Dallas, Texas.

In May 1974, Unified Promotion notified World Convention that its annual allotment would be cut in half to $15,000 per year. Although Allan Lee and others on the Executive Committee protested this cut, the allotment remained at $15,000 or less for the next several decades. To offset this deficit, Lee and others worked hard to increase the World Convention endowment from $40,493 in 1972 to $621,100 in 1991.

Ninth Assembly, Mexico City, July 30-August 4, 1974.

The Stone-Campbell Movement first came to Mexico through the work of the Christian Woman's Board of Missions (CWBM) that began the support of the work of Merritt L. Hoblit in Cuidad Juarez, Mexico in 1895. Others, like Bertha Mason, joined that mission that soon moved to Monterrey. By 1900 the first church was formed with Mexican leadership. Thomas Westrop (1837–1909) and his wife Francesca Barocio (1853–1910) translated hymns into Spanish, began schools, and expanded the mission northward. During the Mexican Revolution (1910–1917), American missionaries fled Mexico, leaving evangelists like Felipe Jimenez to lead the Monterrey churches. The CWBM moved their mission to central Mexico by 1919, moving toward indigenization of the work. By the 1960s Mexican leaders developed a "Revolutionary Plan for Evangelism, resulting in 290 baptisms and a new church in Mexico City. In 1963, the churches formed La Asociacion de Iglesias Cristianas Evangelicas (Disicplos de Cristo), or AICE, the Association of Evangelical Christian Churches (Disciples of Christ).

In addition to the constant financial challenges facing World Convention, the October 1973 oil embargo caused a worldwide financial crisis that affected attendance at the Mexico City, Convention. However, the greatest difficulty with the Mexico City assembly was the initial failure of World Convention to consult and coordinate with La Asociacion de Iglesias Cristianas Evangelicas (Disicplos de Cristo), or AICE. Eufrasio Perez Lopez, the Executive Secretary of AICE, says in a letter that those churches only heard of the choice of Mexico City indirectly and that ". . . we are forced to decline such a distinguished honor" because of lack of personnel and finances, and because "all elements that would take away from us all control of the Convention."[32] However, after Laurence Kirkpatrick met with the Executive Committee of AICE, they did extend an invitation to come to Mexico City and were intimately involved in program planning. Allan Lee, President J. Daniel Joyce, and First Vice-President Daniel Lopez de Lara, along with many

volunteers among the Mexican Christians, worked to produce the meeting in Mexico City.

The Convention opened on Tuesday evening at the National Auditorium with the tradition pageant of flags. President J. Daniel Joyce spoke on the Convention theme, "Emmanuel –God With Us," in a sermon laced with jokes. Over 4000 were in attendance from several countries, including 100 from Australia, but

1974—Translation in Mexico City

---

[32] Letter to William J. Nottingham of the United Christian Missionary Society, January 7, 1971.

the vast majority were from the United States. Several hundred college students came as part of the Phillips University Orchestra, the Milligan College Choir, or as part of several youth choirs from American congregations. This was the most liturgical Convention, with many prayers read in unison from the bilingual program, and the most musical assembly yet. Plenary addresses were in English with about two hundred Spanish speakers hearing translation through headphones.

Another series of study breakfasts met in various locations on Wednesday, Thursday, and Friday morning. Afterward on those mornings, George Sweazy, Professor of Homiletics at Princeton Theological Seminary, gave a series of three lectures as the Bader speaker on Contemporary Evangelism. Walter D. Bingham of the United States preached at the morning assembly at the Hotel Maria Isabel ballroom on Wednesday. The All Nations Luncheon followed with over 1400 in attendance. That afternoon Ballet Folklorico gave a performance for convention goers. That evening American Congressional Representative Edith Green and Mexican pastor Sergio Garcia Romo each spoke on "The Christian Witness and World Issues."

Richard Crabtree, minister of First Christian Church in Canton, Ohio, preached Thursday morning. That evening Professor Leander Keck of Emory University lectured on the place of Scripture, focusing on the positive results of biblical criticism. Friday morning, Mrs. Luis Parrilla of Argentina spoke on "Christian Family Life." The evening sermon was by Ron M. O'Grady of the Christian Conference of Asia.

Saturday morning, August 3, saw four concurrent breakfast sessions for Women, Men, Youth, and Ministers. "The Church Witnesses to the World" was the theme of the evening session, with Ernest T. Campbell, minister at Riverside Church in New York, as preacher.

Because of space limitations, three consecutive identical communion services were held Sunday morning at the Fiesta Palace Hotel ballroom, at 8, 9:30, and 11 a.m.

Again, there were no resolutions at this assembly. There were, as usual, several opportunities for tours before and after the Convention.

Although press coverage was positive, this was the least documented Convention. Also, Mexico City was a very American Convention as far as speakers and attendance. There were worship leaders from several countries, but seven of the ten plenary speakers were from the United States. With only two hundred Spanish speakers present, it was certainly the lowest attendance from a host country.

World Concerns

At the Mexico City Convention, W. Barnett Blakemore was elected President, with the next Convention planned for the United States, perhaps preceded by the Disciples General Assembly. When the plans for connection to the General Assembly fell through, it was decided to have the Convention in Hawaii. Blakemore passed away suddenly on May 2, 1975. First Vice-President Richmond Nelson of Jamaica declined the presidency, feeling that the office should be held by an American. After a search, Forrest D. Haggard, minister of the Overland Park Christian Church in Kansas was elected.

From October 10 to December 12, 1975, Allan Lee made a tour around the world on behalf of World Convention. The trip included stops in Honolulu to meet with the local planning committee, in New Zealand where he spoke at the Annual Conference of the Churches of Christ, in four cities in Australia, then Singapore, India, and to Nairobi for the Fifth Assembly of the World Council of Churches.

At the World Council Assembly in Nairobi, the Council on Christian Unity of the Christian Church (Disciples of Christ) in the United States and Canada, along with other national Disciple bodies formed the Disciples Ecumenical Consultative Council, primarily to appoint official representatives to international bilateral theological dialogues and ecumenical bodies. The creation of the Disciples Ecumenical Consultative Council raised questions about the status of World Convention as a Christian World Communion. Paul A. Crow, Jr., President of the Council on Christian Unity and the General Secretary of the Disciples Ecumenical Consultative Council initially felt that World Convention should no longer be invited to the annual meeting of the Secretaries of Christian World Communions (where World Convention had been a charter member) now that Disciples had a more official body to represent them. After much discussion, the Secretaries invited both groups to their meeting which they have attended annually ever since. In the same way, the World Council of Churches recognizes both organizations, saying, "The Disciples of Christ/Churches of Christ have two international bodies that serve different goals and that operate with different styles: the World Convention of Churches of Christ (WCCC) and the Disciples Ecumenical Consultative Council (DECC)."[33]

---

[33] See https://www.oikoumene.org/en/church-families/disciples-of-christ-churches-of-christ

Anniversary and New Frontiers: Honolulu, Kingston, and Auckland

1980 marked the fiftieth anniversary of World Convention, so it seemed appropriate to hold the assembly in the fiftieth of the United States (or in the words of the *Australian Christian*, "Hawaii Five-O"). It was the first time the United States had hosted the Convention since 1947 in Buffalo. The death of W. Barnett Blakemore had cast a pall over Convention planning, but Forest Haggard did a marvelous job of organizing and promoting the Convention. Morning sessions were held in the ballroom of the Sheraton Waikiki Hotel and the evening sessions in Blaisdell Arena that seated 8800.

Tenth Golden Anniversary Assembly, Honolulu, United States, July 15–20, 1980

The assembly opened Tuesday evening with the traditional parade of flags, this time from the 60 countries that had Stone-Campbell churches. One feature of the Convention was an emphasis on its history with two or three presenters each night sharing personal reminiscences of attending earlier assemblies. Over 7000 were there from fifteen countries to hear President Forest Haggard speak on the Convention theme, "Sharing the Word With the World." He concluded by saying, "We have a Word to share with the World. It is the historical Word of faith in Jesus Christ as Lord and Savior. It is the corporate Word as evidenced in the family of faith. It is the Word made flesh in us."

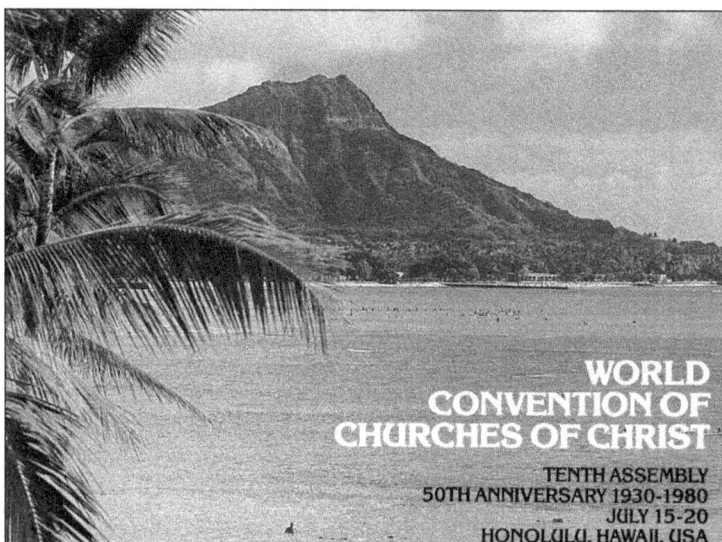

Postcard from Honolulu Convention

Wednesday, Thursday, and Friday mornings began with Study Breakfasts. However, unlike earlier Conventions, these were not so much studies of theological topics, but Bible studies using a printed "Exploring the Bible Guide" that Convention leaders hoped would find widespread use in churches after the Convention. Each of those days the Bible studies were followed by plenary sessions where Alan Walker, the World Evangelism Director of the World Methodist Council, gave a series of three Bader Lectures on Contemporary Evangelism. Walker noted the changing face of world Christianity by stating, "The West is now the toughest mission field in the world." Wednesday morning's sermon was by Kiyo Kamikawa of Japan.

At the evening session Wednesday, Kenneth L. Teegarden, President and General Minister of the Christian Church (Disciples of Christ) in the United States and Canada gave a greeting along with Leonard G. Wymore, the Convention Director of the North American Christian Convention. Wymore's greeting indicated the increased presence of speakers and leaders from the Christian Churches/Churches of Christ at the Honolulu Convention. Wymore also served as the Platform Manager of the Honolulu Gathering. Local pastor Abraham K. Akala gave the sermon that evening.

One feature of every session was the special music provided by the 200 member Convention choir, and by several youth choirs, church choirs, and bell choirs, including the Impact Brass and Singers of Ozark Bible College. Most moving was the performance by the Handbell Choir of the Woodhaven Learning Center, comprised of developmentally challenged youth and adults.

Thursday morning, the Moderator of the Christian Church (Disciples of Christ) and the Past President of the North American Christian Convention each brought greetings, followed by E. LeRoy Lawson of Central Christian Church of Mesa, Arizona speaking on "Toward a New Reformation." That afternoon was the Youth Beach Party (a first for World Convention). In the evening, Russell F. Blowers, minister of the East 91st Street Christian Church in Indianapolis, spoke.

Friday morning's sermon was from another Indianapolis preacher, Thomas G. Benjamin, Jr. of Second Christian Church. That evening, President elect Richmond I. Nelson of Jamaica spoke on "The Living Word for a Dying World."

Saturday morning saw four concurrent sessions. The World Christian Women's Fellowship celebrated its twenty-fifth anniversary with a presentation by Gloria Santos, President of the Asian Church Women's Conference. The Men's meeting consisted of seventeen small discussion groups looking at the meaning of the word "ministry" and at what it means to be a lay minister. Allan Walker spoke at the Minister's Pension Fund breakfast, "In season and out of season, we just go on doing what John Wesley so beautifully describes again and again: 'We offer people Christ.'" George Earle Owen, who spoke at the 1930 World Convention Youth Banquet, was the speaker fifty years later at the Youth Session. Saturday evening was the All Convention Luau with 2400 present for great food and local entertainment.

Sunday morning was the traditional closing communion service outside at the Waikiki Shell. Allan Lee spoke on "The Contagious Spirit."

1980—Honolulu Woodhaven Bell Choir

Sam Catli of the Philippines, Victor and Nellie Smith of England, Robert D. Ray, Mary Louis Rowland, and Rosa Page Welch of the United States received World Convention Citations. As usual there were pre and post-convention tours of the South Pacific and Asia. A small Golden Anniversary medallion was struck and made available for purchase as a souvenir of the Convention.

As mentioned above, the most noticeable aspect of this assembly was the presence of those from the Christian Churches/Churches of Christ on the program, including notable leaders like Paul Bajko, Russell Blowers, Dennis Fulton, Marshall Hayden, LeRoy Lawson, Sam Stone, Leonard Wymore, and others. Most of the local leaders providing arrangements were from the Christian Churches/Churches of Christ. Their presence reflects the determination of the leadership of World Convention to not allow the recent division between Disciples and Independents in the United States to sway the Convention from its purpose of being inclusive of all segments of the Stone-Campbell Movement.

Eleventh Assembly, Kingston, Jamaica, July 18–22, 1984

In the years leading up to the Kingston assembly, Allan Lee travelled extensively, promoting the Convention, connecting the churches internationally, and attending ecumenical meetings like the Secretaries of Christian World Communions and the Sixth Assembly of the World Council of Churches in Vancouver, Canada.

In 1976, the Disciples of Christ in Jamaica had invited the World Convention to meet there in 1984. Therefore there was much time to prepare. This was to be a historic assembly since it was the first to meet outside of the United States, Canada, the United Kingdom, and Australia. Richmond I. Nelson, the President, had served for years on the Executive Committee of the World Convention, had twice been President of the Disciples of Christ in Jamaica, and in 1973 was President of the Jamaica Council of Churches. He and other Jamaican leaders were determined to have an ecumenically welcoming assembly.

Disciples had been in Jamaica since 1858 when the American Christian Missionary Society began support of the work of Julius Oliver Beardslee (1814–1879) a former Congregational minister in Jamaica. During his six years of work, supported by both the ACMS and British Churches of Christ, eighteen mission stations were established with 721 members. However, when the Christian Woman's Board of Missions sent William H. (1842–1938) and Martha Jane Williams to take over the mission in 1876, they only found five small churches. Later the leadership of W.K. and Anne Azbill helped stabilize the mission and led to growth, so that by 1926 there were twenty-five churches with 3,606 members, several schools, and twenty-three Jamaican pastors. In 1929 the Jamaican Association (later Synod) of Christian Churches began, led primarily by local leaders, so that when the missionaries were forced to leave during the Great Depression, the churches continued. The Association supported the ecumenical United Theological College of the West Indies and was also one of the earliest members of the World Council of Churches.

One new aspect of the Kingston Assembly was a multi-year project establishing a medical and dental clinic at Oberlin High School where President Richmond I. Nelson was Principal. Coordinated by the World Convention and by Overland Park Christian Church in Kansas, the clinic was dedicated during the Kingston Assembly.

One concern in planning for Kingston was the lack of hotel space. In addition to the hotels, attendees were housed in college dormitories and in private homes. Several hundred from the United States came to Kingston and were housed during the convention on the cruise ship Victoria.

The assembly opened Wednesday night, July 15, 1984 at the National Arena with over 2000 present from twelve nations. After the pageant of the flags, Richmond Nelson spoke on the convention theme, "Chosen to Do His Work," saying, "The emphasis in the Scripture is on the divine initiative. The truth is, that left to us, the task may not be undertaken at all. It is the bewildering fact of the Christian experience that we who are nobody have been made somebody by God. We are chosen to serve this present age."

On Thursday and Friday mornings, Eugene A. Nida of the United Bible Societies, the foremost authority on Bible translation, gave the two Bader lectures on evangelism. He enthralled the audience with many examples of the difficulty of translation but also challenged them to translate the gospel into life. "There's enough gospel preaching in one week to save the whole world, just not enough gospel living!" Thursday evening, Robert C. Shannon, minister with the Christian Churches/Churches of Christ in Largo, Florida, in "The Partnership We Share," spoke honestly of the challenges and hopes regarding Christian unity. "I would be unrealistic if I said that the things that divide us are not significant; they are. But there are towers of unity rising above our differences."

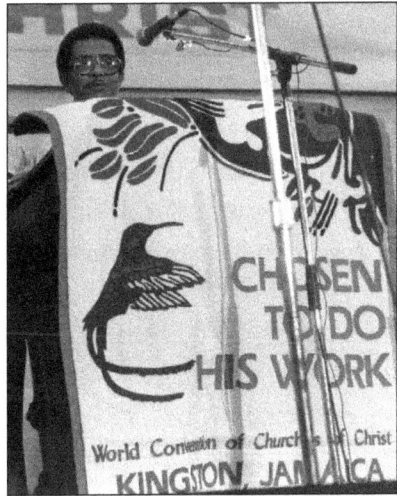

1984—Richmond Nelson

He went on to highlight World Convention as one of those towers of unity. Roy G. Neehall from Trinidad, former General Secretary of the Caribbean Council of Churches, gave his own challenge in Friday night's sermon, "Christ calls us to challenge the traditions that deny fulfillment of the purpose for which God sent his Son." Neehall called on Christians to admit their own affluence and to ban poverty.

As in Honolulu, Saturday morning brought four concurrent sessions. Elizabeth Alvarez de Barbosa, past President of the Puerto Rican Christian Church Convention, addressed the World Christian Women's Fellowship. Eugene Nida spoke at the Men's Fellowship. Roy G. Neehall spoke to the Minister's Pension Fund Breakfast. The youth had their own session. Saturday night was the Jamaican cultural night with performances by folk dancers and singers. At the Sunday morning communion service, Eugene W. Brice, Disciple minister in Kansas City, called the congregation to learn to pray in other languages, the languages of need and hurt, the languages of pain and protest.

Citations were presented to Douglas Nicholls of Australia for his work among aboriginals, Larimer and Gwen Mellon for their medical service in Haiti, Leonard Wymore for his years of leadership of the North American Christian Convention, and to Jamaican Keith Goldson.

With only five plenary speakers, there were fewer program participants than previous assemblies. However, this had its benefits as Mark Taylor wrote in the *Christian Standard*[34], "The World Convention's program is more relaxed than some, providing ample time to see sights, enjoy meals, and spend time with others who are attending."

Between the Kingston and Auckland Conventions, the General Secretary and Executive Committee continued their ongoing ecumenical work and their efforts to promote unity among all those of the Stone-Campbell heritage. One example of those efforts was the appointment of Leroy Garrett from the American a cappella Churches of Christ as a member of the Executive Committee. Garrett also led a study session in Auckland.

12th Assembly, Auckland, New Zealand, November 2–6, 1988

In 1844, Thomas Jackson from Scotland arrived in Nelson and established the first Church of Christ in New Zealand. In 1846, he and others formed a church in Auckland. From these beginnings other churches were planted, so that by the 1880s three district conferences were established that employed evangelists in their districts. By 1901 the first Dominion Conference met in Wellington. By 1905 there were 50 churches with 2400 members.

New Zealand churches began the College of the Bible at Glen Leith, Dunedin in 1927, with A.L. Haddon (1895–1961) as its

---

[34] *Christian Standard* (October 14, 1984), 3.

long-time principal. The school trained ministers and other workers until in closed in 1971. These churches always took the movement's emphases on evangelism and unity seriously, establishing
missions around the world.

1988—Lyndsay Jacobs

But it was in the area of ecumenism that these Associated
Churches of Christ in New Zealand churches had influence beyond
their numerical size. They were founding members of the National
Council of Churches in New Zealand, had attendees at meetings
of the World Council of Churches, and were members of the Joint
Commission on Church Union that included Congregationalists,
Methodists, Presbyterians, and Anglicans.

In 1988, there were 42 congregations of these churches with
fewer than 3000 members total. Their willingness and ability to
host a World Convention is a tribute to their commitment to the
Stone-Campbell Movement and its emphasis on the unity of all
Christians. Key to a successful Convention was the work of hundreds of volunteers led by President Lyndsay Jacobs, an educator,
ecumenist, and editor of *The New Zealand Christian.*

The Auckland Town Hall was the venue for the Assembly, which began Wednesday evening, November 2. The traditional parade of flags was of the twenty-one countries present, not of all countries where there were Stone-Campbell Churches. The crowd of less than 2000 knew they were in the South Pacific when they received a welcoming ceremony from 21 of the Maori people in traditional dress, followed by a welcome from the mayor of Auckland who gave welcoming words in the languages of Samoa, Tonga, Tokelau, and the Cook Islands. Lyndsay Jacobs spoke on the Convention theme, "Turning the World Upside Down" (from Acts 17:1-9), literally inverting a large map of the world so that "Down Under" became up top. He said, "This is the company of reconciliation where people live in unity with each other, in harmony with their world, and within the purposes of God. Here the world has been turned upside down—and people are truly standing on their feet."

On Thursday and Saturday morning were study breakfasts with a new emphasis. Since 1988 was the two hundredth anniversary of the birth of Alexander Campbell, attendees used a study guide prepared by Hiram J. Lester, professor at Bethany College, to look at Campbell's life and influence. Friday evening a birthday party was held for Campbell at the Sheraton Auckland Hotel, with Lester and Ron O'Grady of New Zealand speaking of Campbell.

Thursday morning's session was the first of three Bader lectures by American television preacher and bestselling author Lloyd John Ogilvie, minister of Hollywood Presbyterian Church. His theme Monday was power in evangelism, "Power is given by God to fulfill the work he has called us to do." That evening, Rod Huron, Director of the North American Christian Convention, called on attendees to have the Spirit of Jesus, asking "What would happen if we were to see people not as they are but as they could be? Seeing people as they can be, that is the Spirit of Jesus."

Three simultaneous breakfasts were on Friday morning. Speaker Alison O'Grady of New Zealand urged those at the World Christian Women's Fellowship to "feast at the banquet of life." At the men's breakfast, John O. Humbert, President and General Minister of the Christian Church (Disciples of Christ) honored Garfield Todd for his work in Southern Rhodesia. Lloyd John Ogilvie, at the Pension Fund breakfast, urged his fellow ministers to lead their congregations to deploy their members in Christian service. "Are we prepared to maintain a passionate commitment to the God of Christian unity?" was one of the questions asked by evening speaker Bill Tabernee, Principal of the Federal College of the Bible in Australia.

Saturday, after the study breakfast, Ogilvie gave another Bader lecture on hope and evangelism. "With such a hope we are able to go forth into the world and be willingly expended for the sake of people in the name of Christ who gives us hope." That evening was the ecumenical service of the Convention with greetings from Baptist, Roman Catholic, Methodist, Presbyterian, Salvation Army, and Friends leaders. American Disciple Joan Campbell, Executive Secretary of the United States Office of the World Council of Churches, gave a stirring sermon on unity, ending by saying, "What we do now determines what is to come, so we must bear witness to God's love and God's future, a task that is large while we are small, ordinary people called to an extraordinary task. Once again, Christian unity must be our pole star. Once again, we must turn the world upside down. So we must forbear each other in love, and let us in eagerness maintain the unity of the Spirit in the bond of peace. Love so amazing, so divine, demands our soul, our life, our all."

In Sunday's communion sermon, Lloyd John Ogilvie reflected on the experience of the last few days in Auckland, "Our renewed experience of Christ's love during this Convention gives us new passion to reach the millions who do not know Him, and new power to serve wherever people suffer." The 1800 present communed with cups handmade by Lorraine Jacobs.

1988—Maori children

The congregational singing, choir of New Zealand singers, and visiting bell choirs blessed the assembly. Several received citations, including Ray and Marjorie Blampied of New Zealand. There were tours before and after the Convention. It was in many ways it was the best organized of the Assemblies, and was clear testimony that any nation, regardless of the size of its population or number of churches, could host a wonderful World Convention.

Repetition and Innovation: Long Beach and Calgary

After the Auckland Convention, Allan Lee announced his intention of retiring as General Secretary effective at the next Convention. Lee served twenty-two years in that position, planning five assemblies, representing World Convention at scores of international ecumenical gatherings, and visiting Stone-Campbell churches throughout the world. His greatest legacy was the phenomenal increase in the endowment, allowing World Convention to survive and thrive in difficult economic times.

13th Assembly, Long Beach, California, USA, August 5–9, 1992

Hal Watkins, President of the Board of Church Extension of the Christian Church (Disciples of Christ) in the United States and Canada, was chosen to serve as President of the Long Beach Convention. His experience as a pastor in Alabama and Arizona and his many years at Church Extension, gave him many contacts among the Disciples and the Christian Churches/Churches of Christ in the United States. Watkins had family in both of these groups and saw World Convention as a family union for the entire Stone-Campbell Movement.

The Convention began Wednesday evening, August 5, at the Terrace Theater of the Long Beach Convention Center. Preceding the pageant of flags, the Thailand Folk Troupe performed the Thai flower dance of blessing. As at Honolulu, the Impact Brass and Singers of Ozark Bible College performed. Hal Watkins gave the address on the Convention theme, "God's Dominion: From Sea to Sea," making a cleaver play on French and Spanish words, "From Si to Si." Asking if God truly has dominion, he stated, "For those of us who believe Jesus is the Christ, the answer is a resounding 'Yes!'"

Thursday and Friday mornings saw Bible study breakfasts on the Convention theme. Leroy Garrett had prepared the brief Bible study booklet used by small groups of six to eight adults. Youth had their own session with music, drama, choirs, talks, and "rapping." One new feature at Long Beach was a series of dramatic performances by a group from Central Christian Church, San Antonio, Texas. After their performance in the morning session, Fred B. Craddock, Professor of New Testament and Preaching at Emory University, gave the first of three Bader lectures. Many considered Craddock, a member of the Christian Church (Disciples of Christ), as the finest preacher in the United States. He did not disappoint, speaking of the simplicity of faith and confession in a sermon entitled, "The Journey is Long, Pack Simply." Thursday evening, citations were presented to Dean Harrison, Rod Huron, William Howland, and Joan Campbell of the United States, and to Ron and Alison O'Grady of Australia. In his sermon, Allan Dunbar of the Bow Valley Christian Church in Calgary, Canada, called on the attendees to be "people who are mature and friendly."

Bible study, a drama on the life of Jeremiah, and congregational singing preceded Craddock's sermon, "Jesus is Here, but the Storm Continues," on Friday morning. That evening, the Presidents of three Stone-Campbell Colleges in Southern California—Pepperdine, Chapman, and Pacific Christian—gave greetings. "In as much as we express God's love to our neighbors, his dominion will be felt from sea to sea." These are words from the Friday evening sermon by Keith Farmer, Principal of the Churches of Christ Theological College in Australia.

The World Christian Women's Fellowship, the Minister's Pension Fund Breakfast, the Men's Fellowship, and a youth session all met concurrently on Saturday morning. Joan Brown Campbell, General Secretary of the National

1992—Thai Drama of prodigal daughter

Council of the Churches of Christ in the USA, spoke to the WCWF. Craddock spoke at the minister's breakfast and Leroy Garrett at the men's fellowship. The youth experienced a Galilean breakfast by the sea, where performers in costume enacted the life of Jesus. Saturday night there was a dinner in honor of Allan and Mildred Lee, with performance by the Thai Folk Drama group and an address of appreciation from Bert B. Beach, long-time secretary of the Christian World Communions from the Seventh Day Adventist Church.

Fred Craddock spoke again at the Sunday morning communion service. One highlight of that service was the moving ceremony of installation of Lyndsay A. Jacobs as General Secretary and Lorraine M. Jacobs as Associate General Secretary.

In terms of program, Long Beach broke little new ground, looking very much like the programs of the previous four Conventions. Attendance was under 2000, almost all Americans. Of the fifty named participants in the program, forty-two were from the United States, with the others from Australia, Jamaica, New Zealand, and Canada. The Convention also had a budget shortfall of almost $39,000.

Although the Jacobs were chosen as General Secretaries at Long Beach, it would take some time for them to move from New Zealand. The Executive Committee also decided to move the office of World Convention to Nashville, Tennessee, where it would be housed at the Disciples of Christ Historical Society. To ease those two transitions, the Executive Committee appointed former President Forrest Haggard as interim General Secretary until the Jacobs began their work in Nashville in January 1993.

Lyndsay and Lorraine Jacobs

The Jacobs came to World Convention after careers as educators in New Zealand. Both had rich ecumenical experience. Lyndsay had served on the Program Committee for the 1980 Convention, was President in 1988 in Auckland, and had served on the Executive Committee ever since. Lorraine was an accomplished artist who had created the communion ware for the Auckland Convention. Each was talented but together they were a formidable team, Lyndsay's insight and organizational skills complimented by Lorraine's social skills and creativity.

Their appointment was historic in many ways. They were the first couple to truly share the calling of General Secretary, although Mildred Lee had worked as office manager with Allan. They were the first from outside the United States to lead World Convention, and thus the first not from the Christian Church (Disciples of Christ). This brought challenges but also opportunities. Since they were not from any of the three North American "streams" of the Movement, they brought a new perspective that could not be accused of bias toward one group. As members of a united congregation in New Zealand, they had experienced the joys and difficulties of a wider Christian union firsthand.

The Jacobs threw themselves immediately into the work, in spite of the challenges of moving half way around the world, entering a new culture, and setting up a new office. Most Sundays found them worshipping three times—with Disciples, Christian Churches, and Churches of Christ—as they built new relationships to promote World Convention. They initiated a program of "Friends of World Convention" to give financial support from several countries, publishing a quarterly "Christian Friends" newsletter to keep them informed. They attended international ecumenical meetings, visited churches in dozens of states, and planned for the next Convention in Calgary. This activity took its toll on Lyndsay's health, leading to hospitalization just two months prior to the Calgary Assembly. Thankfully, he recovered in time for Calgary.

14th Assembly, Calgary, Canada, July 30-August 4, 1996

Churches that would become part of the Stone-Campbell Movement initially came to Canada through Scotch Baptists, Haldanes, and English Baptists who emigrated from Britain. John R. Stewart an immigrant from Scotland began the first church in Prince Edward Island in 1810 (a year before the Campbells began the Brush Run Church in the United States). These churches eventually developed their own identity as Churches of Christ or Disciples of Christ, organizing their first Cooperation Meeting in Norval, Ontario in 1843. Ontario was the numerical center of the movement and many from there planted churches in the Western Provinces during the last half of the nineteenth century. Perhaps the most influential leader in that century was David Oliphant, Jr. (1821–1885) who had studied under Alexander Campbell at Bethany and shaped the churches as an evangelist and an editor.

By the late 1880s there was a growing division in the Canadian churches similar to that in the United States. In 1901 there were 67 churches with 4711 members associated with the Disciples of Christ and 11 churches with 750 members associated with Churches of Christ. The Disciple churches organized the All-Canada Committee in 1922 to coordinate the work. In 1927 they formed the All-Canada College to train ministers; it later became a college without walls that provided funds for study at any university or seminary. When the Christian Church (Disciples of Christ) was formed in 1967, these churches became a regional expression of that church. They now number 22 churches and 1800 members.

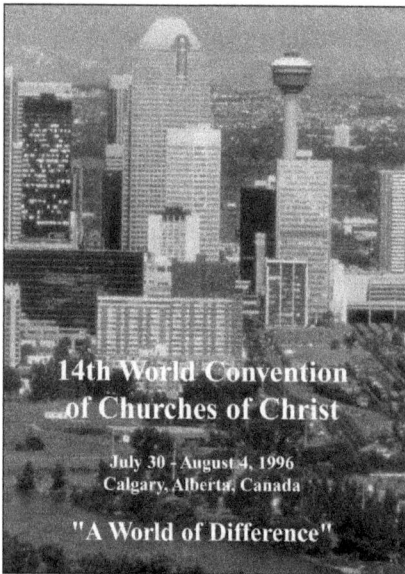

14th World Convention
of Churches of Christ

July 30 – August 4, 1996
Calgary, Alberta, Canada

"A World of Difference"

1996—Calgary program

Churches of Christ also spread into the Western Provinces in the 20th century. They founded Western Christian College in Saskatchewan in 1945, but after moving twice, the school closed in 2012. Great Lakes Christian College in Ontario is also associated with this group. The group includes 138 churches and over 7000 adherents. Christian Churches and Churches of Christ also have 62 churches with 9400 adherents in Canada. The influential Alberta Bible College, founded in 1932, is associated with them.

All three groups joined in the arrangements for the Calgary Assembly. The Western Canadian Christian Convention and the All Canada Assembly of the Disciples met jointly with the World Convention. After serving as President of the World Christian Women's Fellowship and for two decades on the Executive Committee, Marj Black became the first woman to be President of World Convention. Her extensive contacts in Canada and throughout the world made her an effective leader of the Calgary Assembly.

With the theme, "A World of Difference," the Convention opened Tuesday night, July 30, 1996 at the Corral at Stampede Park. The parade of flags, representing the 159 countries of the Stone-Campbell Movement, were led by a procession of Canadian Mounted Police. Over 2000 attendees joined in singing a hymn composed for the occasion by David L. Edwards. Marj Black, dressed appropriately in her cowboy hat, gave the presidential address, "With God, We Can Make a World of Difference." Drawing on her own family and church experiences, she urged hearers to trust that God can make a difference in their lives and in the world.

One new feature of Calgary was a Youth/Young Adults Convention for high school and college students. While other assemblies had youth programs, this was a complete parallel Convention, running from Wednesday to Saturday, with Bible studies, worship, recreation, field trips, and concerts. There was also a Children's program with field trips during the day and a Vacation Bible School in the evenings.

Wednesday morning's adult session featured the Bader lecture in a new format. Instead of a single speaker, there were three Bader lecturers at Calgary from three countries. After each lecture, listeners broke into small groups for discussion and then reassembled for a brief question and summary time with the speaker. Wednesday's speaker was Cynthia L. Hale, Senior Minister of the dynamic Ray of Hope Christian Church in Georgia, U.S.A. Calling on all Christians to be evangelists, she said, "Energetic, creative evangelism programs need to be developed through which persons may channel their evangelistic zeal . . ." Wednesday evening's speaker, John Killinger, Professor at Samford University in Alabama, wondered if we were limiting Jesus because we thought we knew him so well.

Thursday morning brought the first of several dramatic presentations on the scripture text by Clarice Friedline. Gordon Moyes, Superintendent of the Wesley Mission (Australia's largest Christian welfare service) gave the Bader lecture on "Proclaiming a World of Difference With Concern." Proclaiming a new evangelism with social responsibility, he said, "When we preach that Christ can change individual lives, we must also address the capacity of Christ to change communities and corporations."

Another innovation at Calgary were two workshop sessions on Thursday afternoon. Attendees could choose one of eight workshops on stimulating topics like the Stone-Campbell heritage, Bible translation, use of the internet, or reports on the church in various parts of the world. Twenty teachers from seven countries led the sessions.

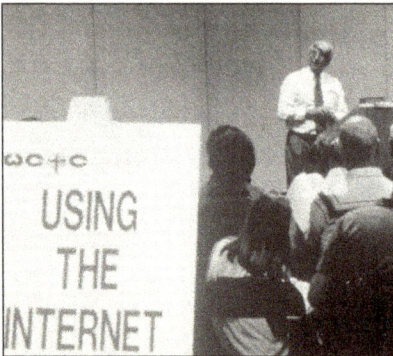
1996—Neil Topliffe on Using Internet

On Thursday evening, Rubel Shelly, minister for the Woodmont Hills Church of Christ in Nashville, brought a moving lesson on Christian unity. "Unity is not ours to create but ours to receive as God's gift of grace." Shelly's presence was significant since he was an influential leader in a cappella Churches of Christ. Like Carl Ketcherside and Leroy Garrett, who had spoken on earlier Conventions, Shelly's life epitomized the shift from sectarianism to openness to other Christians that a cappella churches were experiencing. The congregational singing at the Thursday evening service and the closing worship of the Convention were a cappella to recognize the growing involvement of this group in World Convention. One attendee from New Zealand said "many judged it to be the musical highlight of the Convention."

Andrew Bajenski from Warsaw, Poland, stated, "True godliness makes a world of difference in a person's life, in evangelism, and in this world," in his Bader lecture Friday morning. Over 900 attendees went by bus to Rafter 6 Ranch to have a western style picnic on Friday afternoon. That evening they were blessed by speaker Derik Davidson, who had served as Moderator for the United Church of Jamaica and the Cayman Islands. He spoke of the threat of the current world situation but focused on the promise of "a more comprehensive unity which will produce community with a human face where basic needs are satisfied and diversity is recognized and celebrated."

Concurrent brunches for men, women, and clergy were held Saturday morning. That evening, Ian Allsop, National Secretary of the Churches of Christ in Australia, challenged the congregation to have their mind renewed with new insights, new vision, and new relationships. Dick Hamm, General Minister and President of the Christian Church (Disciples of Christ) in the U.S. and Canada preached at the closing communion on Sunday. "Our mission is not to make the world the same, and certainly not to make it like us. But we are called to appreciate the world's differences and to lead the world toward being one in Jesus Christ!"

Those at Calgary left for tours or to return home with their souvenir communion cups, precious memories, and new relationships. They had been part of the most innovative Convention to date. The Jacobs, Marj Black, and others on the program committee had brought in the new elements of a Youth Convention, contemporary Christian songs (some sung a cappella), small group discussion of the Bader lectures, and topical workshops. There was a greater variety of presenters on the program with fewer from the United States and a clearly increased presence of women.

Sites of the next two Conventions were announced at Calgary: Brisbane, Australia in 2000 with Ron Brooker as President, and Brighton, England in 2004 with David Thompson as President.

Creativity and Tradition: Brisbane and Brighton

After the Calgary Convention, the Jacobs were busy with the everyday ministry of connecting the Stone-Campbell churches globally. One way of publicizing this everyday fellowship or continuing convention was through two email newsletters they initiated, *World Convention NewService* that told news of our churches worldwide, and *World Convention Journal* that focused on the ministry of the Convention. They also had a website developed for World Convention. *Christian Friends*, a print journal begun in 1993, was changed to *World Christian* in 1998, with a circulation of 10,000 mailed to eighty-seven countries by 2010. They wrote two helpful brochures—"Our Story" to briefly tell the history of the global movement and "Who Are We?" to tell common characteristics of the movement. They created a program of World Convention Ambassadors to promote the ministry in several countries.

The Jacobs also made personal contact through church visits and displays at the major gatherings of Stone-Campbell Christians in the United States and other countries. In 1997, they set up their display at the Abilene Christian University Bible Lectures, the first time World Convention was represented at a gathering of a cappella Churches of Christ. They traveled to Israel, Kenya, and Turkey to connect our churches and to scout possible sites for future Assemblies.

One ongoing meeting that grew out of World Convention was the Stone-Campbell Dialogue in the United States. At a World Convention Executive Committee meeting, Dick Hamm, President and General Minister of the Christian Church (Disciples of Christ), commented that American Disciples had international dialogues with many Christian denominations but no dialogues with those who shared a common heritage. As a result of that comment, in 1999 a small group from each of the three streams in North America—the Christian Church (Disciples of Christ), Churches of Christ, and Christian Churches/Churches of Christ began to meet "to develop relationships and trust within the three streams of the Stone-Campbell Movement through worship and through charitable and frank dialogue 'that the world may believe.'" The Stone-Campbell Dialogue is not part of World Convention, but it is an expression of its mission as a catalyst organization to promote internal unity in the Stone-Campbell Movement. The General Secretary of World Convention has been a part of every meeting of the Dialogue.

In addition to this connection work inside the Stone-Campbell Movement, the Jacobs continued to represent the Movement ecumenically. Either Lorraine or Lyndsay attended meetings in Istanbul, Geneva, Windsor, and Jerusalem of the Secretaries of Christian World Communions. Lyndsay was an invited observer to the Eighth Assembly of the World Council of Churches in Harare, Zimbabwe (World Convention General Secretaries had attended every assembly but one since the Council began). He reported, "In our family of churches there are those whose commitment to the World Council of Churches is very strong and others who will never be able to support such an organization. However, my overall feeling was that everybody within our family—both supporters and opponents of the World Council of Churches—would have been glad about the general direction the council was taking." While in Zimbabwe, Lyndsay met with several churches and leaders, including Garfield and Grace Todd.

15th Assembly, Brisbane, Australia, August 2–6, 2000

World Convention returned to Australia thirty years after the Adelaide assembly. As with the other Australian assemblies, there was a groundswell of national volunteers to make sure all was ready for the international visitors. President Ron Brooker was a business-man who had spent his life in service to the church. He even took courses at the Church of Christ Theological College to prepare himself for his Presidential role. Along with others, he prepared a forty-seven page Local Action Guide for those preparing for the Brisbane Convention.

This well-organized assembly opened on Wednesday, August 2, 2000 at the Brisbane Exhibition and Convention Centre, with the theme, "Gathering Under the Cross." Earlier that day, over 270 participated in the

2000—Marj Dredge

first Global Leaders Forum, discussing worldwide issues. That evening the session opened with greeting from a leader of the aboriginal first peoples of Australia. Over 3000 from thirty-two countries heard the opening message from American televan-gelist Robert H. Schuller, founder of the Crystal Cathedral in

Garden Grove, California. Speaking on "His Cross—Our Crown," Schuller said, "We have to learn to die as church and be born again as mission."

Ron O'Grady of New Zealand gave the most moving presentation of the Convention on Thursday morning. Drawing from his work in founding the global movement to end the sexual exploitation of children, he said, "to those who have been abused as children the church must apologize. They were victims but often were made to feel shame or guilt for what happened. We commend them to the love and example of Jesus." At the end of his address children came forward and led the assembly in "Jesus Loves Me." His presentation was so powerful that it was published in the *Christian Standard* in the United States and in *Reform—the Magazine of the United Reformed Church* in the United Kingdom.

Thursday morning attendees had a choice of twelve seminars on a variety of topics. That afternoon was the first offering of Ministry Tracks in five areas—worship and creative, youth ministry, women's ministry, care ministries, and missions. Offered Thursday, Friday, and Saturday in seven modules, there were thirty five sessions in all. Sam Stone, editor of the *Christian Standard*, spoke that evening on renewal, rebuilding, and restoration. "We get wrapped up in our own little world—our church, our college, our publication, our part of the universal church—and we forget that there are a lot of other believers out there. Some of them think differently than we do; they talk differently, look differently, sing differently, and live differently, but they are still our brothers and sisters. God can renew us all, under the cross."

Friday morning's speaker, Carol Preston of Australia, issued a call to "pass through the fires of transformation that are inherent in the spiritual path of maturing, the path which Christ himself followed." Three more ministry track session followed that morning and afternoon. The evening speaker was internationally known writer Leonard Sweet who challenged listeners to please God, not themselves. He even issued cards to the audience that changed "Please, God" (our usual appeal in prayer) to "Please God!"

2000—Brisbane wall hanging

"We tend to think of missionaries as those few adventurous souls that local congregations send out to distant places. What we all know to be the truth, but are afraid to think about too much, is that the local church is a missionizing, evangelizing, witnessing community for the gospel." So said Alvin Jackson from National City Christian Church in Washington, D.C., Saturday morning's speaker. His session was followed by ten more seminars in the morning. Well-attended lunches for Men, Ministers, and Women preceded two more rounds of ministry tracks. Saturday evening was the highlight for many Convention goers with a gospel concert with several performers including Australian jazz legend James Morrison. Saturday was an event filled last full day of the Assembly.

Over 3500 were present for the a cappella worship at the communion service Sunday morning. Graham Agnew of the Northside Church of Christ in Sydney sent them out with the charge to "communicate with clarity, change with sensitivity, celebrate with intensity, and challenge with integrity."

In all a total of over 4500 attended at least a portion of the Convention, hearing singing groups from Zimbabwe, Vanuatu, the Philippines, and Australia, and being blessed by the performances of the Thai Folk Dance Group. The visual arts were represented by a patchwork wall hanging with squares depicting the work of the congregations throughout Australia. Other World Convention traditions continued—uplifting speakers from many nations, the parade of flags, citations, and souvenir communion cups (in this case, communion trays hand-painted by Dot Brooker). However, this assembly, like the one at Calgary, will be remembered for its innovations like the Global Leader's Forum and the ministry tracks.

Several important projects were begun between the Brisbane and Brighton assemblies, including moving the office to a new location in Nashville and revising the World Convention constitution. "Sharing the Stories, Strengthening the Witness" was an ambitious undertaking to briefly describe the manifestations of the Stone-Campbell Movement in every country. Clint Holloway joined the World Convention staff primarily to work on the project. Improvements to the World Convention website were made with the help of webmaster Ed Dodds. Through the suggestion of supporter Don Breiby, World Convention called on Christians worldwide to pray for Christian unity daily at 11:11.

To connect churches and represent our movement, the Jacobs visited Thailand, Japan, the Philippines, Brazil, the United Kingdom, Australia, New Zealand, Canada, Germany, and Switzerland. In addition to attending forums, lectureships, conventions, and assemblies in the United States, they also celebrated the 200th anniversary of the Cane Ridge Revival in 2003. After eleven years of energetic and creative service to World Convention, the Jacobs made plans to retire after the Brighton Assembly. After a search was made, Jeff Weston of Australia was appointed to begin as the new General Secretary, effective January 1, 2005.

16th Assembly, Brighton, England, July 28-August 1, 2004

"Founded in Christ—Building for Tomorrow," was the theme of the Brighton Convention, the first to be held in the United Kingdom since Edinburgh in 1960. President was David M. Thompson, lecturer at Cambridge University, with years of ecumenical experience who had been one of the leaders of the union between the Churches of Christ and the United Reformed Church in the United Kingdom. Those congregations who did not join that union—the Fellowship of Churches of Christ in the United Kingdom—were also involved in planning the Brighton assembly.

2004—Musa Dube

Before the assembly, on Wednesday, July 28, 2004, 125 leaders met at the Global Leader's Forum, where reports of the churches in various parts of the world were given. That night was the opening session with the traditional parade of flags from the forty-one countries of attendees. Martin Robinson, minister with the Fellowship of Churches of Christ, spoke on "Seeding Goodness," saying, "The future is shaped by committed minorities; single generations have the capacity to change the world. Why not this generation in the 'West'?"

Thursday morning began with Bible study on 1 Corinthians 3:10–17, led by Australian Merrill Kitchen who urged her listeners "to be active proclaimers, not passive consumers." Her presentation was followed by study in small groups by the participants. One new feature at Brighton was the choice of twelve "Tools for the Task" groups, focused on particular ministries, that met in three sessions on both Thursday and Friday. That evening, after music from the Mountain Mission School Choir from the United States, speaker Verna Cassells of the Caribbean and North American Council for Missions said, "The gospel is about unity and peace. We must be evangelists for unity and peace as a means of abounding in grace."

Musa Dube of the University of Botswana led the Bible study Friday morning. "Just as barriers had to be broken down between Gentile and Jew, reconciling all God's people for mission remains vital," she said. That afternoon the revised Constitution for World Convention was approved. Joel Edwards, General Director of the Evangelical Alliance of the United Kingdom, challenged attendees to "take the gospel from pulpit to pavement" in the evening session.

Saturday morning the Bible study was led by American Gene Boring of Brite Divinity School. He highlighted three images of church—temple, priests, and community. This was followed by a choice of twelve seminars on ministry and mission. Luncheon meetings for the World Christian Women's Fellowship, men, and ministers followed. After lunch was a choice of ten more seminars. Saturday evening was a set of performances that highlighted the cultures of the United Kingdom.

At the closing communion service on Sunday, President David Thompson called for renewal, "We have to move forward. A key to all building for the future is renewal. And renewal involves repentance and forgiveness." The Convention closed with attendees in unison saying a prayer from Vanuatu:

O Jesus, be the canoe that holds me in the sea of life;
Be the steer that keeps me straight;
Be the outrigger that supports me in time of great temptation.
Let your Spirit be my sail that carries me through each day.
Keep my body strong, so that I can paddle steadfastly on,
In the long voyage of life.

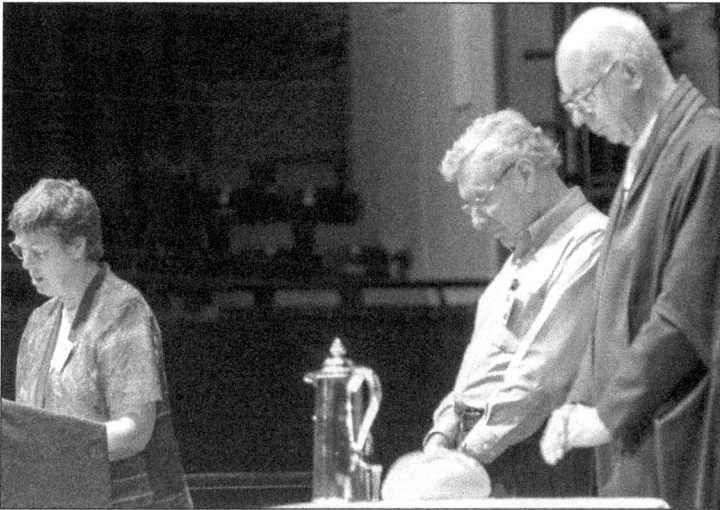

Lyndsay and Lorraine Jacobs and David Thompson

Brighton will be remembered for traditional hymn singing, encouraging speakers, more inclusion of women on the program, and the ecumenical breadth of presenters. There were youth sessions and children's programs. Citations were given in two categories, the Allan and Mildred Lee Awards for service to the church and the Garfield and Grace Todd awards for service to the wider community. The "Tools for the Task" and seminar sessions were well received and welcome additions to the traditional program. Attendance was around 1500, lower than previous assemblies.

After Brighton, the transition was made to the new General Secretary, Jeff Weston. Weston had served as a missionary in Papua New Guinea, in several Churches of Christ in Australia, and as the Executive Director of the Australian Churches of Christ Overseas Mission Board. He and his wife Rosemary moved to Nashville in October 2004 and had three months of working with the Jacobs until he became General Secretary on January 1, 2005.

Old Country and New Country: Nashville and Goiania

Jeff Weston faced several serious challenges in his first years as General Secretary. One was a financial shortfall from the Brighton assembly and the expenses of moving from Australia. Second was the difficulty of obtaining permanent residency status in the United States because of the restrictions imposed after the attacks of 9/11/2001. The third challenge was organizing an assembly in Nashville. Although president Robert Wetzel gave much leadership in the planning, it still fell to Weston to negotiate with the convention center, hotels, and transport companies. In reality, Weston served both as General Secretary (renamed as Executive Director) and as local organizer for the Nashville Convention.

In addition he had the usual travel schedule for World Convention, with trips to Italy, India, Zimbabwe, Korea, and Brazil, in addition to travel to meetings in the United States. He represented World Convention at the first Global Christian Forum in Limuru, Kenya in 2007.

17th Assembly, Nashville, United States, July 30-August 3, 2008

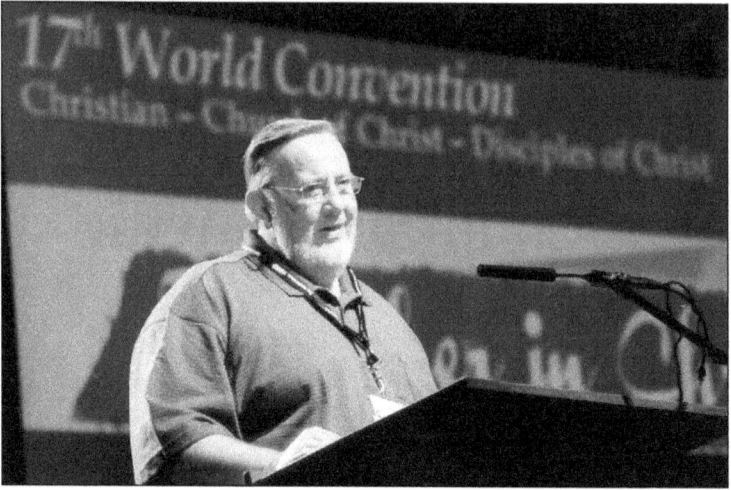

2012—Jeff Weston

The Nashville assembly marked many firsts for World Convention. C. Robert Wetzel, President of Emmanuel School of Religion, was the first to be President of World Convention from the Christian Churches/Churches of Christ. It was also the first assembly to be held in a stronghold of a cappella Churches of Christ, with over 100 congregations of that fellowship in Nashville.

The local planning committee enlisted many volunteers to insure a smooth-running assembly. Of great help financially was the partnership provided by many colleges, ministries, and other entities of the three North American streams of the movement. An extensive range of exhibitors also provided funds alongside the registration fees from 1600 attendees.

Two significant meetings took place before the Convention opened. Global Women Connecting (the new name for the World Christian Women's Fellowship) held a retreat July 28–30. Ninety leaders from eleven countries shared in the third Global Leaders

Forum on July 30. There they received resources from several publishers and ministries.

The assembly opened Wednesday night, July 30, 2008 at the Nashville Convention Center with the traditional parade of flags. Worship at the assembly was led by Ken Young and the Hallel singers, a group that skillfully blended contemporary and traditional songs sung instrumentally and a cappella. Opening night speaker was Cynthia Hale, pastor of the Ray of Hope Christian Church, one of the largest congregations of the Christian Church (Disciples of Christ). Speaking on Christian unity, she emphasized that "It's not that complicated," saying "We don't have to manufacture unity. We just have to maintain it."

An exciting new offering at Nashville was a series of early morning worship choices Thursday, Friday, and Saturday. Attendees could experience their choice of contemplative, contemporary, blended, or a cappella worship. Or they could chose to worship with African, Brazilian, or Hispanic Christians. After morning worship on Thursday, Rhonda Lowry, professor of Spiritual Formation at Lipscomb University in Nashville led the Bible study. She was the first woman from a cappella Churches of Christ to speak at a plenary session of World Convention. On Thursday, Friday, and Saturday afternoons, a choice of forty-six workshops were offered by fifty presenters from all over the globe. Thursday evening's keynote was from the best known minister among American Christian Churches/ Churches of Christ, Bob Russell of Southeast Christian Church in Louisville.

2008—Nashville Communion service

Friday morning's Bible teacher was Ajai Lall of Central India Christian Mission. That evening, speaker Mike Cope of Highland Church of Christ in Abilene called on listeners to affirm the unity brought by and expressed in their common baptism, saying "Water is thicker than blood." Saturday, B.J. Mpofu, incoming President of World Convention from Zimbabwe led the Bible study. That evening was a concert featuring Australian guitarist, Tommy Emmanuel.

The communion service Sunday was historic in many ways. It served as the inauguration of the "Great Communion," a series of communion services to be held throughout in world in 2009 to commemorate the "Declaration and Address" written by Thomas Campbell in 1809. The communion table at the Nashville Convention was one used at the 1909 Centennial Convention; the communion chalice and plate were those used by Alexander Campbell (all of these items were borrowed from the Disciples of Christ Historical Society in Nashville). In his communion sermon, Robert Wetzel reminded attendees of their heritage in the Stone-Campbell Movement, especially of the gift of weekly celebration of open communion. "We come to the table, kneel, and confess before the cross of Christ that we are all sinful, we are all in need." This was followed by a moving communion meditation by Executive Director Jeff Weston.

There were children's and youth programs at Nashville, the youth program featuring Ajai Lall, Jeff Walling, and Virzola Law as speakers. The youth program was held in a church eighteen miles from the Convention Center which prevented the youth from being part of the larger program. Nashville also kept features of earlier Conventions such as citations and tours.

A disconcerting note from Jeff Weston in the printed program at Nashville was his statement, "At the time of writing we are unsure of our tenure with World Convention. We have been unable to secure Permanent Residency in the US so we have to depart the country by August 2009." Financial challenges also faced the Convention. Although the Nashville assembly had a surplus financially, the world financial situation greatly affected World Convention. When B.J. Mpofu was chosen to be the President, the intent was for the next assembly to be in his native Zimbabwe. However the collapse of the Zimbabwean economy made that impossible. Christians in Brazil stepped in and agreed to host the next Global Gathering (a new name for the Assemblies) in Goiania, Brazil in 2012.

The move of the Westons back to Australia left a leadership void. The Executive Committee appointed William H. "Bill" McDonald, retired minister of the Christian Church (Disciples of Christ) as interim Executive Director in August 2009. Reduced fundraising for several years coupled with the great global recession beginning in 2008 had reduced gifts to World Convention. The Executive Committee instructed McDonald to cut the World Convention staff to the Executive Director and a half-time office manager. McDonald also made promotional trips inside the United States and represented World Convention at the Secretaries of Christian World Communions meeting in Canterbury, England.

Effective February 1, 2010, Gary Holloway became Executive Director, the first from a cappella Churches of Christ to have that role. Coming from a background as a college and seminary teacher, Holloway had less experience with World Convention than his predecessors, having served on the local planning committee for the Nashville Convention. However, Office Manager Julia Keith, who had worked alongside the Jacobs and Jeff Weston, provided much needed continuity and orientation.

Holloway immediately began planning for the 2012 Goiania Convention, alongside President B.J. Mpofu and local organizer Victor Hugo de Queiroz. In addition to a planning trip to Brazil, he visited Australia, New Zealand, Poland, and South Korea and promoted World Convention at convocations, assemblies, conventions, lectureships, and churches in the United States. He also attended the annual meetings of the Secretaries of Christian World Communions, and along with 260 other world religious leaders was invited by Pope Benedict XVI to pray for peace in Assisi, Italy in October 2011.

The 18th World Convention, Goiania, Brazil, July 25–28, 2012

Logo for Goiania Gathering

In 1948, Lloyd David Sanders, a recent graduate of Johnson Bible College and Phillips University, and his wife Ruth came to Brazil as missionaries. Settling in the Goias area, they began to plant churches. When the new capital of Brazil, Brasilia, began in 1960, the Sanders secured one of the first church sites. As a result of their more than 70 years of work, there are over 300 churches in Goias and the Federal District, led by Brazilian ministers. More than thirty other direct support missionaries associated with Christian Churches/Churches of Christ have worked in Brazil. The vast majority of churches today have Brazilian pastors who are organized as the Ministerial Council of the Churches of Christ in Brazil. Today these Brazilian Christian Churches number 440 churches with a membership of over 90,000. The Brazilian churches send out and support Brazilian missionaries in Mozambique, Angola, Guinea-Bissau, Mexico, Portugal, the United States, and India. In 2011 Brazilian Churches partnered with Korean churches to plant the Korean speaking Bom Retiro church near Sao Paulo.

American Churches of Christ first came to Brazil through the work of three missionary couples who settled in Mata Grande in the late 1920s. With Brazilian workers, they planted several churches in Ceara, Rio Grande do Norte, Paraiba, and elsewhere. However the missionaries and a majority of churches joined the Assembly of God in 1935.

Churches of Christ returned in 1956 through the work of Arlie and Alma Smith in Sao Paulo. By 1961, fourteen families joined them, planting a dozen churches and preaching on several radio stations. From 1967 to 1970 over one hundred missionaries came to Belo Horizonte, planting churches there and eventually in Recife, Brasilia, Salvador, and other cities, so that today there are around 160 churches with 22,000 members.

Since the 1960s the Christian Church (Disciples of Christ) has sent fraternal workers to minister in three Brazilian churches that are ecumenical partners: the United Presbyterian Church of Brazil, the Association of the Methodist Church in Brazil, and the Evangelical Congregational Church of Brazil.

All of these churches participated in the Goiania Gathering but almost all the planning was done by the Ministerial Council of the Churches of Christ in Brazil. They produced an assembly that was very much Brazilian but open to the world, the first World Convention to be held in South America and the first to be held in two languages since Mexico City in 1974. However planning did not always go smoothly. Just three weeks before the Assembly, the Convention Center that was to be the venue became unavailable. The assembly was moved to the Igreja Videira (Vineyard Church), a recently remodeled church with two large auditoriums, classrooms, and meal spaces that proved to be a much better venue than the Convention Center.

One pre-convention program was a forum held the day before in Brasilia, the capital of Brazil, 120 miles from Goiania. There the focus was on Portuguese language missions throughout the world with reports from Cape Verde, Sao Tome and Principe, Macau, Guinea Bissau, Angola, East Timor, Mozambique, and Portugal.

The Goiania Assembly began Wednesday evening, July 25, 2012 with greetings from B.J. Mpofu, introducing the theme, "Sharing the Love That Unites." Worship was again led by Ken Young with musicians from Brazil and the United States. Young and his colleagues spent much time in arranging praise songs that could be sung congregationally in Portuguese and English simultaneously. Many remarked that the enthusiastic and sincere praise of the Brazilian Christians was the highpoint of the Convention. That evening's speaker was Jerry Taylor, professor at Abilene Christian University, United States. Speaking on 2 Corinthians 9:6–15, he spoke of God's indescribable gift of Christ and how that gift calls us to be generous to others.

Thursday morning, Kang Pyung Lee, President elect of World Convention, left behind his planned presentation and instead gave a moving personal testimony of what God had done in his life. This was followed by another uplifting address given by Waina Tedesco, the first woman consecrated to the office of pastor of the Churches of Christ in Brazil. Thursday, Friday, and Saturday afternoon there were choices of nineteen classes with a variety of topics and teachers. Afterward were the opening sessions of Global Women Connecting and the Youth Congress. Brenda Etheridge, pastor of Unity Christian Church in Michigan spoke on "Christ Heals Our Divisions."

Australian Andrew Menzies, Principal of Churches of Christ Theological College, creatively presented the familiar passage of the Samaritan women from John 4:1–26, Friday morning. Dynamic young Brazilian minister David Livingstone followed with a rousing call for his generation to continue the faithfulness of their predecessors. That evening, Edson Gouveia, well-known and respected speaker among many Christian groups in Brazil, gave an impassioned call to repentance. On Thursday and Friday nights, the speaking sessions were followed by late-night concerts by popular Christian artists.

Since the Convention was meeting in a church needed by its congregation on Sunday morning, the closing communion service was held Saturday night after a full day of sessions. Samuel Twumasi-Ankrah of Ghana and Roberto Fife of Portugal spoke in the morning. That afternoon were classes and special outings for Global Women Connecting and the Youth Congress. At the communion service that evening, the elaborate decoration of the communion table with fruits and flowers impressed those from outside Brazil. At that service, Carlos Pinheiro Queiroz, Executive Director of World Vision Brazil and President of the Brazilian Congress of Evangelization, gave a rousing challenge to the audience to express union with all Christians, not just those of the Stone-Campbell Movement.

Some traditions were kept in Brazil. Citations were given, including a new award named for long-time treasurer of World Convention Rick Reisinger and his wife Denise. Other long standing practices were omitted such as the parade of flags and the souvenir communion cups. Attendance was over 3000, the largest since Brisbane. Overall, it was a great step for World Convention into another culture. As with previous assemblies, many attendees felt the greatest blessing was sharing communion with local churches on the Sunday following the Convention.

After Goiania, Holloway began to work with President Kang Pyung Lee to plan the next Assembly to be held in Seoul, South

Korea in 2016. He also continued to make trips within the United States and to other countries to promote World Convention and to represent the Stone-Campbell Movement ecumenically. One of those trips was to the Tenth Assembly of the World Council of Churches in Busan, South Korea, in October 2013. President Kang Lee at first opposed Holloway's attendance, then gave support, then (unknown to Holloway or anyone at World Convention) led a protest in Busan against the World Council of Churches. As a result of this serious misunderstanding of the purposes of World Convention, the Administrative Committee asked Lee to resign as President.

East and South:
Damoh and Manzini

When the World Convention board (Executive Committee) met in Nashville in April 2014, it happily received a generous invitation from the churches in India for the next Global Gathering of the World Convention to be held in New Delhi, January 12–15, 2017. Ajai Lall was elected President and began the organizational work for the assembly. The International Conference on Missions, led by Executive Director David Empson, partnered with World Convention for the event, providing program ideas and promotion.

The Stone-Campbell Movement has existed in India for over 135 years. In 1882 the Foreign Christian Missionary Society and the Christian Women's Board of Missions, both from American Disciples, sent eight missionaries to Bombay (Mumbai): Greene L. (1846–1906) and Emma (d. 1922) Wharton, Albert (1847–1922) and Mary Kelly Norton, Ada Boyd (d. 1915), Laura Kinsey (d. 1926), Mary Graybiel (1846–1935), and Mary Kingsbury (1857–1926). They soon moved the mission to Harda and were joined by other missionaries in the Disciples India Mission, establishing schools, clinics, publishing houses, and orphanages. By 1907 there were eleven new mission stations and fifty-nine additional missionaries. Through the India Christian Missionary Society, they developed Indian evangelists like Hira Lal (1875–1955) and his wife Sunarin Bai (d. 1952) in Mungeli. This began a process of indigenization of the Indian mission, shown by the founding of the India Disciples Church Council in 1915.

Ajai and Indu Lall with Convention

In 1905 Australian Churches of Christ established a mission in Baramati with the Henry Strutton family. Earlier, Australian Mary Thompson served with the Harda mission. Joined by fifteen missionaries and twenty-six Indian evangelists in the 1920s, they formed the Conference of Churches of Christ in West India in 1927. For the next sixty years Edna Vawser (1902–1994) and Hazel Skyce were leaders of the Conference. Today that work is still assisted by Global Mission Partners of the Australian Churches of Christ. In 1925 the Australian Churches of Christ opened the Dhond mission station that included a hospital led by Dr. G.H. Oldfield.

The Foreign Missionary Committee of British Churches of Christ supported the mission of Paul Singh in Daltonganj beginning in 1909. G.P. Pittman soon joined the mission, supported by Australian churches. Two other mission stations were soon opened through the work of indigenous evangelists.

Indigenization continued to grow throughout the 1920s with Indian leaders like Alfred Aleppa (d. 1947) in Damah, Harrison Singh (trained at Hiram College in the United States) at Barela and later others like Luther Shuh, Samuel Massih, and Peter Solomon.

By the mid-1960s the United Christian Missionary Society missions were almost completely governed and supported by Indians.

The process of ecumenical union also grew from the 1920s to the 1960s. Encouraged by the United Christian Missionary Society (UCMS) and by most British and Australian Churches of Christ, the majority of Indian Churches of Christ supported ecumenical cooperation and eventually joined in the formation of the United Church of North India in 1970.

UCMS missionaries Sterling (1886–1928) and Dr. Zoena (1882–1979) Rothermel came to oppose some policies of the Society as discussed in chapter seven. They continued their work in India, but as direct support missionaries, later associated with Christian Churches/Churches of Christ. Some other missionaries followed the Rothermels into direct support missions. Vijai (1933–1993) and Pushpa Lall had served in a UCMS mission but became direct support missionaries. Their son Ajai and his wife Indu started the Central India Christian Mission in 1982 that today serves thousands yearly in evangelistic and compassion ministries. Other new efforts arose like the Benevolent Social Services of India begun in 1970 by Canadians David (1910–1976) and Lois (1916–2006) Rees, who had served in India since 1953. Missionaries from India and from the United States have planted churches in Nepal, Bhutan, Sri Lanka, and Bangladesh.

American Churches of Christ sent the Edward S. Jelley (1878–1962) family to Bombay in 1911. Three other couples soon joined them. Unfortunately, the unity of this mission was broken by controversy over premillennialism. In 1925 the George Desha family moved to Bombay to continue the mission, but soon moved to Darjeeling. They returned to the United States in 1927. Churches of Christ did not return to India until 1963 through the work of Canadians John Carlos (1903–2001) and Myrtle Bailey, first at Shillong, then at Madras. By 1972, with the help of Indian evangelists like the brothers Nehemiah and Joshua Gootnam, over 700 churches had been planted in the area. Indian Churches of Christ established the Madras School of Preaching (now the National Bible College) in 1969. Many short-term workers from the United States came to assist Indian evangelists. Ron and Karen Clayton, missionaries in India for over 30 years, have kept detailed records of congregations and baptisms and list 48,880 Churches of Christ in India with a combined membership of 1,139,562 today.

While planning for the India Global Gathering, World Convention also continued its work in relating to the wider church. The Christian Church (Disciples of Christ) has been involved in ecumenical dialogues for decades, since 1979 through the Disciple Ecumenical Consultative Council. Christian Churches/Churches of Christ and Churches of Christ are quite similar in theology and practice. These two churches have not been involved in ecumenical dialogues partly because of the challenge of representation in a congregationally organized church and partly because of their opposition to or apathy toward a wide ecumenism.

However, in more recent years, both churches are more open to ecumenical engagement. World Convention is the only global organization that can provide them with a seat at the ecumenical table. The Consultation on Believers' Baptism, held in Kingston Jamaica in January 2015 was a historic first for these churches. Although it was not a bilateral dialogue, it did mark the first time that theologians from Christian Churches/Churches of Christ and from Churches of Christ participated in a global ecumenical consultation. Their presence was important since there are significant differences in practice between those churches and Disciple churches, such as in the acceptance of those baptized as infants for membership.

Gary Holloway also represented World Convention at the Secretaries of Christian World Communion meetings in

Amersfoort, Netherlands in 2014, in London in 2015, and in Rome in 2016. He was a guest at the Church of God General Assembly in 2016. He also represented our churches at a special event in Lund, Sweden, sponsored by the Lutheran World Federation and the Pontifical Council for Promoting Christian Unity. This event on October 31, 2016, was a joint prayer service with the theme, From Conflict to Communion, marking the 500th Anniversary of the Reformation with repentance for past divisions and a commitment to search for Christian unity.

World Convention had a booth or a spot on the program at Church of Christ Lectureships, the North American Christian Conventions, the General Assemblies of the Christian Church, and other assemblies in the United States throughout 2014 to 2016, promoting the ministry and the India Global Gathering. Holloway also attended the 2015 Annual Conference of the Fellowship of Churches of Christ in Great Britain and Ireland. He made planning trips to Swaziland and Zimbabwe, in hopes of a future Global Gathering in Africa.

Planning for the New Delhi Assembly was in the capable hands of President Ajai Lall. His wide connections in India and its surrounding nations, as well as in the United States, meant he could enlist many in the planning and programing. Gary Holloway and David Empson made a planning trip to India in April of 2015, viewing possible venues and meeting with church leaders from many Indian states.

Having the Global Gathering in New Delhi was a bold decision in a country where less than 3% of the population is Christian. The hope was that holding the Global Gathering in the capital would encourage the government of India to be more visible in promoting religious freedom.

However, bureaucratic government regulations and unexpected costs led the Indian planning committee to suggest a venue change from New Delhi to Damoh, India. The World Convention board approved this change in September 2016.

The move to Damoh called for great effort from the Indian committee, led by President Ajai Lall. The staff of Central India Christian Mission (CICM), other ministries in Damoh, and many volunteers worked tirelessly to transform the campus of CICM into a welcoming place for over 3000 visitors from 29 countries and 21 Indian states. The hospitality of the Indian Christians was overwhelming, from the gracious welcoming ceremony each person received, to the accommodations and excellent food.

The Gathering began Thursday evening, January 12, with a plenary session held in a beautifully appointed tent, lit by chande-

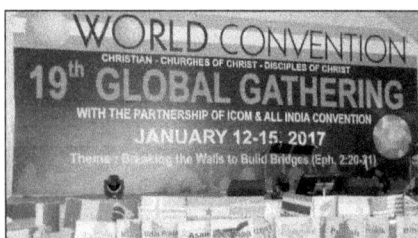

Banner at Damoh

liers, with a large banner behind the stage with the theme, "God Breaks Down Walls to Build Bridges." The parade of flags from the 29 countries and 21 Indian states of those present began the Gathering, accompanied by the song, "He Reigns." Hosts Indu and Ajai Lall welcomed the attendees, followed by a traditional welcome dance by students from the Nursing School of Central India Christian Mission. Government and ecumenical guests gave greetings, followed by citations presented to Robert K. Welsh of the United States, Lyndsay and Lorraine Jacobs of New Zealand, and Leonard W. Thompson of India.

After lively singing, led by Indians, Ajai Lall spoke on the assembly theme, identifying three walls that Jesus came to tear down: the wall between head and heart, the wall between faith and action, and the wall between traditionalism and truth. Brent Liebezeit of Nelson, New Zealand, was the second speaker of the night, giving a rousing call to remember that Jesus is God with us. He ended with an invitation to allow Jesus to lead us into a revolution that takes us beyond borders to tear down walls of guilt, shame, and failure.

"Jah masih ki! That's the Hindi phrase all participants learned on the second day of the Global Gathering. It means, "Praise the Lord!"

And there was much to give praise for on Friday of the Gathering. The day began with a greeting from Richard Howell, General Secretary for Asia Evangelical Alliance (AEA) and Vice President of World Evangelical Alliance. Howell encouraged all present to be part of the Global Christian Forum. His greeting was followed by the plenary session with speakers Jeff Fife of Brazil and Andrzej Bajenski of Poland. Fife urged those present to build bridges to those who do not know Jesus and bridges among Christians. "To build bridges, we must have a servant spirit." Bajenski had a brilliant twist on the Gathering theme, reminding us that there is a good wall, the wall that surrounds the New Jerusalem, with gates that admit the holy people of God into his Presence.

The afternoon provided three concurrent sessions for women, men, and youth. At the Global Women Connecting meeting, Sheela Lall challenged those present to unite to break walls of darkness, hurt, and fear. Abhineeta Matney presented the Aatma Vikas ministry as the service project of Global Women Connecting. David Eubanks and Brent Liebezeit spoke to an overflow crowd of youth. At the men's session, drawing from the story of the woman at the well (John 4), Dave Stewart showed how Jesus educated the Disciples in love. David Henry urged social change brought through seeking guidance from the Holy Spirit.

Julia Keith at Global Women Connecting

Late afternoon brought workshops focusing on unity and mission throughout the world. Before the evening session, there was a cultural program of traditional Indian dance. Evening worship included recognition of long-serving ministers to India. Denford Chizanga brought a message of peace with God in the midst of storms from Mark 4. Usha Rees called those present to bridge to others in love, saying "Stop judging how far people still have to go, and start celebrating how far they have come." Friday was a full day of blessing. "Jah masih ki!"

Saturday morning began with a greeting from Ajay Singh, the state minister, who was honored for his protection of the Christian minority in India. This was followed by a joyful presentation in song and dance by children from the children's home in Damoh.

Radical love seemed to be the theme for the morning session, Josh Howard called all to a renewed Restoration Movement that restored radical love, radical generosity, and radical unity. LeRoy Lawson followed with a reminder that God translated his love into body language through the incarnation and he asks us to embody that same love. With Jesus as the bridge to God, Lawson asked us to be the ramp that leads others to the bridge.

At noon, several persecuted Christians from different areas of India gave their testimony to a small group of those from outside India. One woman told of the attack where she was repeatedly raped and her husband was killed. A man told of being beaten unconscious, only to wake in the hospital to find his wife had been murdered. All because they would not renounce their Christianity. There was even testimony from a man who once persecuted Christians, then became one himself, and now plants churches in northern India. Such stories of faith moved the hearers to tears and to prayers thanking God for the courage of these believers.

Afternoon were the second sessions of the youth, men's and women's fellowships. Lydia Soko from Zimbabwe spoke to on

"Loving the Unlovable" and Esline Toamavute from Vanuatu spoke on "Reaching the Unreached" on the second afternoon of Global Women Connecting, followed by a time of jewelry making and henna tattoos—trade skills learned by students of Aatma Vikas. In the men's session, David Clayton and Vivert Lall eloquently presented on the cost of entering the kingdom and the covenants God has made with his people. Leonard Thompson and Josh Howard spoke to the youth.

In the evening, after a marvelous cultural program of Indian dance, Cynthia Peacock gave a greeting for the Mennonite World Council. Then Dave Ferguson reimagined the Prodigal Son story, helping us to feel the Prodigal's fear of rejection by family and neighbors. He then urged that our churches say, "In this place there will be no rejection," and that they back up that claim by feeling it, telling it, and living it. The picture of a jigsaw puzzle was used by Oscar Muriu of Kenya to reveal the apostle Paul's teaching on gifts and unity from 1 Corinthians 12.

Speakers Ajai Lall, Dave Ferguson, and Oscar Muriu

Just as the puzzle pieces must be different for there to be a picture, so God has given different gifts to each part of the church. This forces us to work together to be the beautiful picture God paints. Muriu brilliantly applied this to the local, national, continental, and worldwide expressions of church. Each has a gift from God that must be used to benefit all.

"Dhanyavaad" That's the Hindi word that sums up the final day of the Damoh Global Gathering. Dhanyavaad means "thank you." And there was much to be thankful for on the last day. The local church in Damoh joined the attendees on Sunday, swelling the crowd to over 3,500, joining in lively singing, insightful preaching, and heartfelt farewells.

Ajai Lall, the President of the Global Gathering, explained the corruption, increased costs, and extortion from the media that made it impossible to have the Gathering in New Delhi as originally planned. The move to Damoh seemed like a series of impossible tasks—finding rooms for the 3258 who registered, providing meals, and creating meeting spaces. But by grace and the hard work of Indu Lall, Lashi Howard, the staff of Central India Christian Mission, and others, God worked the miracle of Damoh. The preacher for the morning, Jeff Vines, told stories showing how only Jesus can explain suffering, meet the deepest desires of the heart, and do for us what we cannot do for ourselves.

As is usual in our Global Gatherings, the highlight was communing through the Lord's Supper with Christians from 29 nations and 21 states of India. Our worship was followed by a fellowship meal provided by the Damoh congregation.

The Damoh Convention was historic in many ways. It was the first in Asia. Those from outside India were amazed at the quality of the preparations made for them—meals where Christ was shared among the nations, the smiles, handshakes, and photo sessions with our Indian brothers and sisters, the encouraging words in music and sermons, and the clear call to tear down walls and build bridges. At the end of each Global Gathering, attendees will call it "the best." But the Gathering in Damoh was without doubt a turning point in making this truly a *World* Convention.

That desire to reflect the churches it serves led the World Convention board, meeting in Damoh, to accept an invitation for the next Global Gathering to be held in Manzini, Swaziland in April 2019. This will be the first Global Gathering in Africa, following the first in Asia and the first in South America.

Past and Future

Looking back at this brief telling of the World Convention story, certain aspects stand out. First are the people of World Convention. We have named the Executive Secretaries, Presidents, speakers, organizers, and a few others. So many more deserve mention, including those from twenty-five countries who served on the board, some for decades like Stephen England, Peter Solomon, David Coulter, Shernett Smith, Carmelo Alvarez, Richard Ziglar, Lester Palmer, Katherine Ann Haggard, Ken Masterson, Doug Foster, Stan Litke, Douglas Dornhecker, and Marj Dredge. Then there are the local organizers and hundreds of volunteers that made each assembly possible. Thousands spent their time and money to attend the assemblies. And thousands through the years have supported the ministries of World Convention with prayers and gifts.

The scope and variety of the programs of World Convention are impressive. Not only the programs of the assemblies with their wide scope of speakers, musicians, dramatic performances, and study sessions, but the ongoing programs of the Convention blessed thousands. The multi-decade study groups drew on wisdom from dozens of countries to produce accessible theological documents. The World Christian Woman's Fellowship (now Global Women Connecting) sprang from World Convention, as did (in a more informal way) the Stone-Campbell Dialogue. World Convention gives all our churches a seat at the ecumenical table, with participation in the Secretaries of Christian World Communions and delegate status at the Second Vatican Council and the Assemblies of the World Council of Churches.

World Convention connects Stone-Campbell churches daily through publications. Through the years these have included printed newsletters and journals like the *World Conventioner*, *Christian Friends*, and *World Christian*. The results of the study program as well as brief pamphlets like *Our Story* have also come from the press. In more recent decades, a monthly email newsletter, *ChristiaNet*, keeps readers informed about the news of the churches and of World Convention. The Convention website, worldconvention.org, also contains news and the profiles of the 199 countries of the Stone-Campbell Movement.

Most of all, World Convention has been and continues to be a ministry of prayer. When Jesus wanted all who believed in him to be one, his first step in accomplishing that goal was to pray (John 17:20–23). Prayer has been a vital part of every assembly and every program every day. World Convention invites all to pray for Christian unity daily.

So there are bright prospects for World Convention. Christian unity is both a gift and a calling from God. Every day there are signs that God is working powerfully among his diverse people so that they may recognize their unity and together share the love of God with others so that the world may believe. Unity and evangelism have always been the hallmarks of World Convention. May they continue to be so in new places and new ways until the day that every knee bows and every tongue confesses that Jesus is Lord.